Stressed-Less
LIVING

Stressed-Less
LIVING

Finding God's Peace in
Your Chaotic World

Tracie Miles

LEAFWOOD
P U B L I S H E R S

STRESSED-LESS LIVING

Finding God's Peace in Your Chaotic World

LEAFWOOD
P U B L I S H E R S

Copyright 2012 by Tracie Miles

ISBN 978-0-89112-335-4
LCCN 2012016102

Printed in the United States of America

Unless otherwise noted, all Scripture quotations are taken from the Holy Bible, New Living Translation, copyright 1996, 2004. Used by permission of Tyndale House Publishers, Inc., Wheaton, Illinois 60189. All rights reserved. Scripture quotations noted NIV are from The Holy Bible, New International Version. Copyright 1984, International Bible Society. Used by permission of Zondervan Publishers. Scripture quotations are from The Holy Bible, English Standard Version® (ESV®), copyright © 2001 by Crossway, a publishing ministry of Good News Publishers. Used by permission. All rights reserved. Scripture quotations noted MSG taken from *The Message*. Copyright 1993, 1994, 1995, 1996, 2000, 2001, 2002. Used by permission of NavPress Publishing Group. Quotations in Chapter Eight were written by Patrick Lencioni, used by permission. Mr. Lencioni is the author of ten business books including the new release, The Advantage: Why Organizational Health Trumps Everything Else in Business, and the national best-seller, The Five Dysfunctions of a Team. He is founder and president of The Table Group, a management consulting firm focused on organizational health. Quotations from *Holman Illustrated Bible Dictionary*, Lifeway and B&H Publishing Group, used by permission.

Published in association with WordServe Literary Group, 10152 Knoll Circle, Highlands Ranch, CO 80130.

LIBRARY OF CONGRESS CATALOGING-IN-PUBLICATION DATA
Miles, Tracie, 1967-
 Stressed-less living : finding God's peace in your chaotic world / by Tracie Miles.
  p. cm.
 ISBN 978-0-89112-335-4
1. Christian women--Religious life. 2. Stress management--Religious aspects--Christianity. 3. Stress management for women. 4. Anxiety--Religious aspects--Christianity. I. Title.
 BV4527.M4395 2012
 248.8'43--dc23

                                                                2012016102

Cover design by Jennette Munger
Interior text design by Sandy Armstrong

Leafwood Publishers is an imprint of
Abilene Christian University Press
1626 Campus Court
Abilene, Texas 79601

1-877-816-4455
www.leafwoodpublishers.com

13 14 15 16 17 / 8 7 6 5 4 3

To my husband Michael,
*whom I've shared the past twenty- two years with and
who has supported me in my calling in more ways than one.*

To my children, Morgan, Kaitlyn and Michael,
*the greatest joys of my life,
who have brought more blessings to my heart than they will ever know.*

To my mother, Barbara,
*the most amazing woman I know,
who has always been my biggest cheerleader.*

Table of Contents

" . . . you are worried and upset about many things,
but only one thing is needed . . . "

—Luke 10:41b–42a NIV

Foreword

by Stephanie Clayton, MEd

I wish I'd had this book the day I walked into the counselor's office. I kept asking myself, "Why am I here?" I had recently completed my master's degree in counseling and been accepted into the doctoral program. Shouldn't I be able to handle the stress-induced panic attacks that paralyzed me and filled me with shame? I wondered what my future would look like. Was I doomed to be dependent on a counselor to manage my stress?

I spent the better part of two years in counseling, dealing with baggage and pain from my past. Heart palpitations, night sweats, teeth grinding, stomach pain, headaches, and depression ruled my days. I was stressed. Facing my past seemed terrifying, my present was uncertain at best, and my future appeared dim. Stress was strangling me and threatened to never let go.

Although I'd studied stress reduction techniques in school, I had not learned to apply them to myself. The demands of life set the bar high and I set the bar even higher. I beat myself up for struggling under the weight of it all. It was not until I completely offered my heart and mind to the Lord, like Tracie helps us do, that healing began to wash over me.

Do you struggle with stress too? Have you tried countless remedies only to end up defeated and overwhelmed? Speaking from a personal and a professional viewpoint, stress can be dangerous. Prolonged stress can lead to high blood pressure, asthma, skin conditions, diabetes, depression, anxiety, and more! In fact, many long-term mental health concerns can be traced back to chronic and unaddressed stress reactions. As a counselor, I work with individuals to help them develop healthy coping skills and stress reactions. We also work to address the issues that lie underneath stress, such as pain from the past, present circumstances, time management concerns, and environmental factors. However, the most important thing we can do while attending to the stress in our lives is to take it to the Lord.

Matthew 11:28 (NIV) tells us, "Come to me, all you who are weary and burdened, and I will give you rest."

Anxious thoughts and tendencies can steal our joy. The Lord, however, came that we might have abundant life. His plan for us includes peace and rest in his presence. Even if all the deep breathing techniques in the world continue to leave us feeling breathless, we can turn to the Lord.

That's why I'm so excited about this book! Tracie shares God's transforming truths with you from a vantage point of having lived each and every word she shares. She's felt bound by stress and life circumstances and understands what stress can do to our bodies. Best of all, she has found freedom in Christ. If you have lived the last few days, months, or even years bound by stress—this book is for you. You will see yourself in the stories Tracie shares, find hope in the Word of God, and be challenged towards growth by the questions at the end of each chapter.

The day my confidence walked out on me, God stayed by my side and did not leave me there alone. He wants to do the same for you, too! If you feel wrecked by stress and circumstances, it's time to move forward and embrace *Stressed-Less Living* in Christ.

Stephanie Clayton has a passion for integrating Bible teaching with professional counseling. She has a master's degree in counseling and a bachelor's degree in psychology. She serves on the Online Bible Studies team and Gather and Grow team with Proverbs 31 Ministries and writes at www.stephanieclayton.org.

Introduction

Do you ever feel like life has you by the jugular, choking out your every breath? Do you wake up each morning feeling exhausted emotionally and physically, wondering whether you can make it through another demanding day? Do you ever struggle with feelings of hopelessness or helplessness?

Do you sometimes feel like you are a ticking time bomb, liable to explode or implode if one more stressful thing happens in your life? Do your friends and family walk on eggshells around you, in fear that they may say or do something that will set you off?

Do you ever wish that you could wake up tomorrow and discover that you have been teleported into a new life or at least a tropical island for a day?

Have you been feeling frustrated, fatigued, frazzled, overworked, overloaded, overwhelmed, or overcommitted? Or maybe all of the above? If you answered yes to any of these questions, then, my friend, you have picked up a resource that might change your life.

Through the pages of this book, you will learn how to recognize the signs of burnout, the symptoms of chronic stress, and the consequences of ignored stress. By pulling out the stress-relief secrets hidden in the Bible, you can soak in down-to-earth encouragement and biblical practices that can truly relieve stress from everyday life experiences such as work, home, marriage, child rearing, addictions, health, and the economy. It will help you leave your chaotic world filled with worry and anxiety and enter a new world filled with unshakable joy and abundant peace.

Many people are under the impression that the Bible is not a resource for handling stress, much less for finding stress management tips, simply because the word "stress" is not a biblical term. Although the word "stress" was not commonly used in biblical times, Jesus referred to this disease consistently through synonyms that can be found in every Bible translation and on practically every page. Synonyms such as anxiety, worry, troubles, fears, burdens, anguish, dismay, strain, trials, tribulations, and adversity, just to name a few.

He spoke of the heartache of anxieties, fears, frustrations, and betrayal, the sadness of deceit, the pull of temptation, and the devastation of sin. He tells of difficult circumstances taking place in politics, churches, relationships, marriages, families, parenting, sexual sin, and communities and the world as a whole.

Despite the differences between biblical times and the twenty-first century, the presence of stress and our need for Jesus is the same. The lack of the term "stress" certainly did not keep Jesus from understanding a stressful life or from promising the peace we would need to hear and apply in today's busy, chaotic, stressful world. It didn't keep him from voicing encouragement and reminding us of the hope that is available in him and that is applicable no matter what century we live in. Jesus knew we would be stressed, so he not only addressed it, he provided the solutions for dealing with it.

Jesus teaches us how to celebrate life, despite life. How to find joy, despite circumstances. How to overcome stress, despite the constant balancing act that we all experience. How to not only survive the storms but to stay afloat in the midst of them. From Genesis to Revelation, we can discover infinite suggestions for biblical stress relief if we only seek them out.

Stress is not a sign of the times, it's a sign of life—always has been, always will be. Our stressors may be different today than when Jesus walked the earth, but, nonetheless, the overwhelming sickness of stress is exactly the same.

Maybe you have tried every stress relief tactic known to mankind, to no avail. If so, I pray that you will soon discover that all the stress management tactics in the world cannot hold a candle to the real and permanent stress relief that Jesus offers. His methods have withstood the test of time, used by generation after generation, and he is the only tried, true, and proven stress relief method there has ever been.

If you have been searching for a peace and serenity that seems completely out of reach, maybe you have simply been searching in all the wrong places.

You have not picked up this book by mistake. If you are ready for answers, a fresh start, a renewed spirit and have a desire to live the stressed-less and abundant, joy-filled life that Christ intended for you, I invite you to join me on this journey.

Give it a shot. You have nothing to lose and life to gain.

Chapter One

Discovering the Real Problem

I used to think that my stress was everybody else's fault. For example, if only my boss were nicer to me, I wouldn't be so stressed out. If my company paid me more, I wouldn't be so stressed about money. If my deadlines were not so unreasonable, I wouldn't be stressed. In fact, if I didn't have to work, I wouldn't be stressed at all!

Maybe you can relate to the statements above, but the list of possible reasons that people feel stressed about every day is infinite. If my husband would help me out around the house more, I wouldn't be so stressed when I got home every day. If my husband would love me more or care more about my feelings, I wouldn't be stressed. . . . If I weren't divorced. If my children would stop arguing. If trying to raise godly children weren't so exhausting. If I did not have this health issue. If my loved one was not sick. If my loved one were still alive. If I didn't have to pay bills. If my house didn't need repairs. If I could buy a new home. If my credit were better. If I could land a new job. If I had gotten that promotion I deserved. If the economy hadn't crashed. If terrorism weren't such a threat. If my friend hadn't betrayed me. If that person had not treated me so rudely or unfairly.

Although I have not recited all of these "if's," over the past number of years, a large majority of them have escaped my lips at one time or another. These are just a tiny sampling of the common issues that people face every day that cause overwhelming stress. As we continue to carry out this ritual of reciting our "ifs," we all eventually convince ourselves that other people are the sole cause, and fully to blame, for our stressed-out lives. I spent way too many years stuck in the habit of doing just that.

However, several years ago, my eyes were opened to the fact that I was trudging through my overly busy life feeling stressed and distressed over big and little things all the time. I realized that not only was I stressed but it seemed life had become a job instead of a joy.

Where was the happiness I once knew? Why did I constantly focus on what was wrong with my life rather than celebrating what was good? Why did I allow the actions and behaviors of other people make me feel so afflicted, angry, incompetent, or hurt? When did I become so negative and melancholy? Why had I become such a pessimist lately? When and how had I morphed into such a frazzled woman? Could I ever feel like myself again?

As these questions swirled through my mind like debris caught in the eye of a hurricane, I knew that something had to change; and through God's intervention, I gradually came to understand that what had to change . . . was me. Once I accepted that truth, my overall life improved. I stopped wondering what was wrong with everyone else, my circumstances, and the world and instead began pondering the hard question: "What was wrong with me?"

As strange as it may sound, throughout the years that I endured the lengthy season of extreme stress and anxiety, I was actually blessed with a wonderful life full of family, love, financial security, a good job, and countless blessings. From the outside looking in, my life may have even seemed perfect. But from the inside looking out, the weight of stress was overshadowing my outlook, gradually choking the joy out of my heart, like a tiny but fatal weed wrapping itself around a beautiful flower, slowly squeezing out the fragile life within.

In hindsight, I can clearly see that I was so caught up in my stressors and problems that I was discounting all those blessings and favors from God. I was missing the opportunity to enjoy my life because I was focused on the stress that consumed every waking moment. I had forgotten what it felt like for my heart to feel light and free, detached from all the twisted and dangerous fibers of stress that had become entangled in my existence.

Pure contentment and peace seemed to be a distant memory, impossible to recoup. I felt like a wayward stick in the middle of the ocean, tossed in tumultuous waves that were constantly crashing in from every direction. Just a little stick in a big chaotic world, with no hope of change and no rescue in sight.

I couldn't remember the last time I laughed heartily at a silly movie or lounged on the couch with my children—apart from my laptop—or enjoyed a leisurely walk without my mind trailing off in a dozen directions, worrying about every situation or person that came to mind. I accepted that something was wrong and that something had to change.

Sometimes God allows us to get to the very end of our rope, barely hanging on by one little thread, before he reaches down and pulls us up with one mighty swoop. Why? Because usually when we get to that desperate point of exhaustion, knowing we have tried to fix things on our own without success, that is the time when we fervently call out to God, and he always answers.

In Matthew 5:3, from the passage known as the Beatitudes where Jesus is teaching his disciples, we are reminded of God's desire to rescue us from ourselves. *The Message* Bible translates it this way, "You're blessed when you're at the end of your rope. With less of you there is more of God and his rule." Less of me and more of God is a delicious recipe for change.

The day I found myself clinging on to that last little frazzled strand on the rope of my life, I called out to God as a last resort. But rather than punishing me for not seeking him earlier or ignoring my request for help as I had been ignoring him, God came swooping in like Prince Charming on a magnificent white stallion.

My eyes became focused on the only One who had the answers, the only One who had the power to pull me out of the stress pit I had dug myself into, and the only One who could catch me when I fell off the rope completely. It was as if I had fallen through a looking glass, like Alice in Wonderland, and was able to catch a glimpse of the strange land I had come to live in. I rubbed my eyes trying to decipher what was in front of me. I finally saw my life for what it was, and I was able to understand my problem clearly.

I saw that stress had become the norm for my life, as opposed to the exception. I saw that I was not only stressed every now and then, or over certain anxiety-inducing situations, I was stressed every day, about everything, involving everyone. When I wasn't paying attention, stress had worked itself into every part of my life, like a snagged thread interwoven throughout a satin, hand-stitched quilt, polluting its overall beauty. After seeing my life from God's perspective, I began to long for my old normal back. Not a perfect normal but a normal that did not exist solely on life-robbing stress.

As a result of this vision, and after much prayer, God led me to a new place—a place that required me to step out in humility, swallow my pride, and admit that I had allowed stress to overshadow my faith. I had gradually put God on the back burner as I hurried through my busy days, tripping over one stressor after another. I knew I needed to make a conscious and determined commitment to God, my faith, and myself and stop blaming everyone and everything for my stress. I needed to lay the blame where it really belonged. If I wanted true, lasting change to occur, I needed to focus on changing me first.

What Works and What Doesn't

Before God gave me a transparent glimpse of my life in the looking glass and before I knew the real root of my issues, I was already well aware that all of my former ways of trying to cope with stress had been woefully inadequate and ineffective.

You see, I had tried holding in all my emotions, putting on an iron mask of calmness and strength every morning, but eventually the simplest thing would tip the scale, the weight of the mask would become more than I could bear, and my façade would be blown.

Then I tried just the opposite—airing all my feelings to my friends, family, and co-workers, hoping that complaining and whining all the time would make me feel better and foster some type of external changes in my circumstances. But eventually they would tire of hearing me rant about my problems. In fact, sometimes I even grew tired of listening to myself.

I tried staying mad at people who were causing me stress, hoping that my obvious cold shoulder would somehow influence them to change who they were. But this method only resulted in further tension, strained relationships, and, of course, more anxiety.

I tried being sad, assuming that the people who were causing me stress would feel some sort of responsibility and accountability for my fragile, pitiful state of my mind. I also felt that by being pitiful, my loyal supporters would continue to be sympathetic and continue to always be there for me. I thought that if I elicited sympathy something would change. In fact, I became a pro at throwing pity parties, even when nobody else was invited but me. But, in the same way I would tire of listening to myself whine, I eventually grew exhausted with being sad all the time. It takes a lot of effort to stay negative, and, when it's all said and done, absolutely nothing is achieved.

I tried massages, manicures, pedicures, fancy vacations, days off from work, bubble baths, hot tubs, listening to soft music, reading fiction, studying stress management books, researching the art of balancing life, grown-up time-outs, and all the other common suggestions for stress relief (except yoga, because I am pretty sure that when I was in my mother's womb, God's future plans for me did not include my becoming a pretzel).

I tried shopping therapy, and, although I love the look and feel of new clothes, shoes, and accessories and enjoy looking my best, the temporary thrill of shopping did not cure my stress either. In fact, all it did was increase my debt, which, of course, caused more stress.

For a short time, I even tried having a glass of wine at night after stressful days, in the hopes that my nerves might be settled in doing so.

But all that accomplished was falling asleep too early, having a restless night, and then waking up with a headache the next morning.

Despite all my varied attempts at stress-management methods in my quest to calm my spirit, the sensation of serenity remained a mere fantasy—a mysterious Utopia that could only be found in dreams or movies. So, regardless of all my futile efforts, I would close out each day by cooking and cleaning and tucking my children into bed, before collapsing in bed myself with a knot in my stomach, heaviness in my chest, an aching in my heart, and worries in my head, knowing that tomorrow it would start all over again.

Despite months of trying to make myself feel better, nothing was working. I was so sick and tired of feeling sick and tired all the time! I had become desperate for an answer, and, since it was glaringly obvious that my circumstances and the people in my life were not apt to change any time soon, I realized I was at a crisis point and needed to find out what was wrong. I needed to know what the real root problem was. I needed to do whatever it would take to get control of my stress, before my stress took complete control over my life. You see, I was worried and upset about many things, just as Martha was in Luke 10. I never sat at the feet of Jesus; instead, I felt like the world's footstool. I was running through life too fast to enjoy it, and, even though I was a Christian, I was blinded to the truth that Jesus really was the one and only thing that I really needed.

When I eventually reached that "end of the rope" stage and admitted my need for him, the doors were opened wide for me to meet him. I finally discovered that the only thing I had needed to do all along to attain the peace I so desired was to ask God for it.

When I finally bowed my head and actually asked, his gentle voice fluttered through my spirit like a crisp fall breeze, and the sensation of serenity literally brought me to my knees—partly because I realized how many years I had wasted seeking stress relief in all the wrong places and partly because I was overwhelmed with the realization of how long God had been waiting for me to give him control. I had finally embraced the promise found in Matthew 21:22, which says, "You can pray for anything, and if you have faith, you will receive it." The only "anything" I wanted was peace.

After that God encounter, my prayers became more frequent and consistent. And, over a period of time, God slowly began to lead me down a new and mysterious path. A path laced with insight and understanding. A path dependent on faith and trust. A path that involved some sacrifice but that led me to a place of peace and calmness of spirit that I thought was only feasible for people with perfect marriages, perfect children, perfect careers, perfect finances, perfect health, and perfect, problem-free lives.

I now know that God is not in the business of seeking out perfect people, he is in the business of blessing those who admit their imperfections and weaknesses and embrace their need for him. We are reminded of this truth in Mark 2:17 where Jesus said, "Healthy people don't need a doctor—sick people do. I have come to call not those who think they are righteous, but those who know they are sinners."

Overwhelming stress is as much an illness to our soul, as cancer is to our body. Jesus came to heal not those who were sick with physical illnesses, although he did perform many healing miracles, but to heal those who were sick with spiritual illnesses—including the debilitating disease of stress. Our hearts are sick when they are burdened with stress, and Jesus is the eternal healer of hearts. He came to bring peace to those who long for real, lasting serenity, and not merely the temporary peace the world has to offer. He came to bring peace that, from a worldly perspective, is only a fantasy but, through him, can become a reality.

Since you have chosen to read this book instead of all the other books on the shelves, I would dare to assume that you may be feeling sick with stress, just as I was. You may be drowning in a life overcome by busyness, anxiety, and worry. You may be sick and tired of being sick and tired. And you may just be realizing that you have also allowed stress to become your new "normal," too.

So, sweet friend, if this describes you, today is the perfect day to start anew. Today is the perfect day to humble yourself before your heavenly Father and admit that you have been sick with stress. Today, the doors of

God's peace swing open as he gives you a new glimpse into your life. It may be time for you to bow your head, confess that you have allowed stress to overshadow your faith, and admit that you too are one of those sick and imperfect people that Jesus died for.

Our humility catapults us into the arms of Jesus, where we can allow ourselves to admit that whether or not we feel peace and joy in our hearts is completely, absolutely, unequivocally up to us and us alone. But that takes time.

As my journey progressed from the stress zone to the faith zone, I allowed God's promises to seep into every ounce of my being. I slowly began to understand that *I* was the only person who had control over my mind. *I* was the only person who had authority over the joy in my heart. *I* was the only person who could determine my attitude on any given day. *I* had to choose to be an optimist, despite negative circumstances. *I* had to make a decision to live life on purpose, as God intended, or to just simply be alive. *I* was the only person who could control how stressed I felt.

Even when other people or circumstances were the external cause of stress, only *I* could allow those problems to suffocate my internal peace. Only *I* could grant permission for the flame in my heart to be snuffed out like a candle.

Whatever you are facing, ask God to reveal what the real root causes are for your stress. Ask him for a looking glass glimpse into your life. Is it circumstances, emotions, resentment, bitterness, pain from your past, the hurtful actions of others, or maybe feelings of helplessness or hopelessness? Is it the exhausting task of playing the blame game? Is it wearing a mask that is weighing you down? Have you allowed others to snuff your inner flame? Is it the strain of parenting? Is it addictions to something or someone? Or is it possibly your perspective about all these things?

Take a moment right now to pause and pray for the strength, courage, desire, and perseverance to look deep into your soul and start trying to see the problem for what it really is. Soul searching can be an effective tool when we are trying to make changes in our lives; however, it can also feel like looking for a needle in a haystack. When stress has become our normal, it takes time to discern what is abnormal beneath the surface. It may seem impossible at first, but taking a peek inside our hearts is the first step towards making positive changes in our lives, one stressor at a time.

When God Steps In

One of the countless reasons why I was so stressed all those years was due to a position I held with an international accounting firm. Although my fancy executive job title looked excellent on a resume, especially when followed up by the exhaustive list of all my oh-so-important job duties, it had become one of my biggest stressors, sucking the life out of me more and more every day. Oh, if only I had known then what I know now, but I guess God couldn't have done his best work if I knew all his plans up front.

As it turns out, God had plans to use this lengthy and difficult season of my life to not only lead me away from that career and into an adventure with him but to lay the groundwork for using that experience as the basis for the book you are holding in your hand. Don't you just love it when you can see tangible evidence of God's promises come true, as we are promised in Romans 8:28? "And we know that God causes everything to work together for the good of those who love God and are called according to his purpose for them."

But since I obviously didn't know then that God had a plan and could only see the chaos that I called my present day life, it took me several years to listen to his call and be strong enough in my faith to pursue the career path he had planned for me. So, as I kept God in the wings and strived to climb the corporate ladder, my stress level moved up a few rusty rungs as well.

A few years prior to surrendering my life to God and eventually resigning from my full-time position to serve in ministry, which I will explain in more detail in Chapter Four, the firm had placed a new job requirement into my lap (on top of all the other requirements that already had me stretched to the max). This new job duty required me to assume responsibility for conducting multiple all-day training sessions to employees throughout the firm's southeast offices on a variety of corporate topics.

When I first heard this, my immediate stressor came from the thought of the excessive traveling that would be required, taking me away from my husband and three small children for long periods of time. But my second stressor was what really took a toll. You see, although I always loved to take on new challenges, I felt an immediate sense of paralyzing fear sink into my heart upon learning of what I would soon be expected to do.

Even though I held a top management position, my work style was such that I was perfectly content sitting in the back of the room during an important meeting and soaking in all of the information. Regardless of how many great ideas were swirling in my head, I never felt quite confident enough to air them aloud. I had no intention of taking the risk of being judged, criticized, or ridiculed. I would jump at opportunities to organize and manage projects, meet deadlines, mentor employees, or offer advice or heartfelt counsel to someone privately, but I didn't much care for being center stage or stealing the limelight from a peer.

I was simply more of a behind-the-scenes, task-focused, goal-oriented manager, and not the kind who wanted to be seen and heard all the time. This certainly set me apart from many of the other managers and partners in the firm, whose goal was to always be seen and heard while pursuing their corporate dream, stepping on anyone who stood in their way. So, in the eyes of some, this difference of opinion regarding office politics and self-centered tactics cast an inferior shadow upon me, and that sense of inferiority had gradually splintered my self-esteem.

So, when I was informed that I was going to be training large groups of people, including managers and peers, I wondered whether I was really cut out for it. My heart raced with worry and insecurities, and my mind became flooded with nightmarish visions of accidentally stepping in front of the crowd having neglected to put my clothes on or tripping and falling over a chair on stage while everyone watches me flail through the air with my skirt around my waist or having my mind go blank in the middle of class and looking like a complete fool.

Yet, since I had no say in the matter, I held my head high, put on a mask of self-assurance, and marched forward like a good little soldier.

How precious that experience is to me now as I look back and recognize that, although I simply thought I was being forcefully shoved out of my comfort zone by my employer, God was secretly grooming me for wonderful plans that only he knew about.

You see, each time I stepped in front of an audience to teach a session or a workshop, God was quietly preparing me for a call to ministry. A call that would require me to stand in front of even larger groups of people than at this organization. A call that would require real vulnerability and transparency, without generic scripts or prompts. A call that would push me further out of my comfort zone than I ever thought possible. A call to serve him in the way that he had planned for my life.

With each presentation I conducted, God was building my confidence in speaking and increasing my comfort level in presenting messages on a variety of topics. Until that experience, I had never contemplated doing anything that would put me front and center. But I learned that God's call on our lives will always be something outside of our comfort zones, and sometimes beyond our wildest imagination.

I can now see that all those times when I felt ill equipped and incapable of fulfilling this new job requirement, God was carving out an amazing future for me that only he could have orchestrated. He knew that he was slowly leading me away from chaos, and he even had a divine plan for using my chaotic, frazzled life for his glory.

I thought I was merely living out a normal life as an over-stressed, maxed out, overwhelmed woman juggling work, marriage, and motherhood, and dealing with a variety of unexplainable health problems. I thought I was wasting away in heart, mind, and soul during the years of unrelenting stress that I had been forced to endure. Yet, all the while I was being trained by my real Boss for my real job, which would allow me to be the real me God created me to be.

What happened next was more than ironic—it was actually comical. An opportunity arose for me to teach people about stress management. How could the National Poster Child for the Most Frazzled Woman of the

Year teach other people how to manage their stress? You can laugh now. It was hysterical to me, too.

From Expert to Experienced

Several years passed since I had first learned of that new job requirement. During those stressful years, I had spent a lot of my time leading training sessions. And, as God would have it, public speaking—coaching and training others about not only work-related topics but also about important life management skills—had grown into something I adored doing.

Shortly after I felt God's confirmation that I was to resign from my full-time position to stay at home with my children and focus on discerning his will for my life, God miraculously opened the door for the opportunity to be a contract corporate trainer. How it came about was truly a God thing, but that is a story for another day. I was beyond thrilled to be able to do something that I had grown to love, while enjoying the blessing of working freelance, controlling my own schedule, and having more time for my family. Over the next couple of years, I became an expert in the area of stress management from an informational corporate standpoint.

As a corporate trainer, I taught countless workshops and training courses in many Fortune 500 companies on a variety of topics, including stress-management and life-balance workshops, so my knowledge grew about all the right things to say to employees who were stressed. I knew which activities they could do to create tranquility at home and work. I knew all the breathing techniques, muscle relaxation exercises, and peaceful meditation strategies. I knew the titles of all the best stress management books, the URLs of websites that offered great tips for dealing with stress, and what type of music was most soothing for the mind.

I knew all the right methods to recommend to people for how to manage their specific stressors. I knew all the trendy terms that organizations used when they wanted to encourage their employees to relax their bodies and calm their minds. I knew all the suggestions to help strengthen strained relationships between co-workers and management. I knew how to build stronger teamwork mentalities and reduce stress and anxiety among team members.

I was highly educated, informed, seasoned, and trained in *all* of the worldly ways to deal with stress. Oh yes, this former stress poster child had become a Stress Management Expert, and I had *all* the answers. Or so I thought.

In hindsight, I can imagine God getting a really good 'n' hearty chuckle at my expense as he watched me spin my wheels day after day, trying to teach people how to be stress-free, without ever mentioning the name of my Jesus. I didn't speak of God not only because it would have been politically incorrect but primarily because I still had not fully discovered for myself that he was the only stress management technique that would ever truly work. Even after quitting my job to pursue a call to ministry, I still had not completely figured that out! Have mercy.

God may have been chuckling, or he may have been weeping at my obvious negligence and ignorance of the real answer people needed, including myself. But, nonetheless, God was up to something big, and his divine purpose would soon be as apparent to me as the streaks of morning sunshine that pierced through my bedroom blinds on a bright summer day.

Trust me when I say that even though I had left my full-time, stressful career behind, my life was still very stressed. The stress that was removed from my ten-hour workday was quickly replaced with financial challenges, parenting issues, marriage struggles, economic concerns, worries, discontentment, and sick family members. The irony was that in the midst of my all-knowing, high-and-mighty, stress-expert, corporate-training career of teaching the how-tos and the dos and don'ts of dealing with stress, I had once again become the National Poster Child for the Most Frazzled Woman of the Year. In fact, my middle name could have been changed to "frazzled," because I had become a pro at being a bad example and a stress-hypocrite.

Instead of becoming an expert on stress management in my own life, I had become an expert on using Band-Aids to cover up my on-edge lifestyle, while giving the illusion that I had it all together. Although I was devoted to teaching other people about controlling their stress through worldly measures, I knew full well that I wasn't applying any of them in my own life.

But, even worse, I secretly knew that in addition to not practicing the techniques I was preaching to the secular world, I was also failing to seek peace through my Savior. Rather than turning to God for answers, I turned back to blaming others. Once again, I became sure that it was not my fault I was stressed, it was still everyone else's fault! I was convinced that if I couldn't change what was making me stressed, then I had a right and an obligation to blame my hurt and stress on whomever or whatever was causing it.

But, as God continued to work on my burdened heart, he slowly began to chisel away at my invisible mask of fakeness, which felt like an appendage of my body, making little holes in my spirit that only he could shine through. Once again, I had dug myself a pit and was dangling over it at the end of my rope. I embarrassingly admitted to God that I had again allowed myself to get pulled into a life consumed by chaos and fallen back into the blame game. I needed him to rescue me, and, when I called out, my Rescuer came through, again.

Then clouds burst open and the sun shone down in glorious streaks! All my stress evaporated and holy angels could be heard singing the Hallelujah chorus from the heavens!

No, not really. But in my heart it kind of felt that way. I sensed a sudden change in my spirit, and I knew my heart was on the brink of being transformed. God had been waiting patiently for me to see that he held the answers to the inner peace I was so desperately searching for. He had been waiting for me to seek him and had given me more than sufficient time to discover that all the worldly ways that I had been teaching were completely useless. Not that they couldn't bring temporary relaxation but they would never bring permanent peace.

I simply had been too stressed to listen to God. But, now that I was listening, I embraced the realization that I had the potential, in him and through him, to once and for all overcome the stronghold stress had held over my life for far too long. Without a shadow of doubt, I now knew that I needed to focus on making his peace the pattern of my life instead of living in a pattern of constantly falling in and out of the stress pit every time I experienced life's ups and downs. When true faith and trust in my Savior became a reality in my heart, living less stressed became a reality in my life. It didn't happen overnight, but it did happen. And it can happen for you, too.

You see, when I finally began to assume responsibility for my own actions and feelings and resumed authority over my emotions, I could determine what the underlying causes were for my stressed-out, fragile state of living. I realized that most of my stress was rooted in trying to control circumstances that I had no control over. I was freed from trying to change people that I couldn't change, from attempting to fix things that I had no resources to fix, from focusing on the unfairness of life instead of the blessings that I had been given because of God's undeserved grace, and from worrying over problems that I had no power to remedy. I was wasting infinite amounts of time, energy, and emotion on things that were completely, 101 percent, out of my control!

So if the truth be known, all of my stress was really self-induced; and in all honesty, that is the case for most people—and possibly the case for you. I would be remiss if I failed to acknowledge what you might be thinking right now, after reading that sentence implying that your stress is your own fault: *What? No way! That person / circumstance / wrongdoing / unfairness / hardship / adversity / illness / money problem is the cause of my stress! How dare you insinuate that I am bringing this despair on myself! The nerve!*

Friend, I absolutely understand if you disagree completely and adamantly with the idea that your stress is even partly your fault. Maybe you cannot imagine relinquishing blame of other people or circumstances and taking ownership for your own state of mind. Maybe you truly believe to the depths of your soul that the actions of other people are the root cause of your stress or that the difficult situations in your life, which are not even your fault, are the real culprits. And those feelings are completely and absolutely valid. I would never negate your deepest raw emotions because those feelings are real and, when we have been hurt by people or by life, it's hard to release blame. We feel like we are letting those people or circumstances off the hook, and they don't deserve that type of grace from us. It's hard to push past our emotions and latch onto faith.

I know it's hard, but it is so worth it.

As you continue to read through this book, my prayer is that you will learn to understand and believe without a shadow of a doubt that, despite your valid emotions, raw feelings, open wounds, and heavy heart, you are the only one who has authority over your attitude, your joy, and, yes, even your level of stress.

It is difficult to wrap our minds around that concept, because our flesh wants to blame-blame-blame, our minds want to worry-worry-worry, and our hearts want to hurt-hurt-hurt. But if we are holding onto that hurt, worry, and blame with both hands clenched, then we won't have any hands left to grab on to the peace that God places within our reach.

We have to let go of what is not good for us so that we can grasp the good that he has for us. And stress is definitely not good for us.

A Vicious Cycle

Would you agree that stress is like a never-ending cycle of emotions? As we become consumed with the problems and stressors in our lives, even those we cannot change or fix, we get sucked into caverns of negative emotions that become hard to escape.

The more we worry, the more anxious we feel; the more anxious we feel, the more frustrated we become; the more frustrated we become, the more we want to find someone or something to blame. As frustration builds, we get more and more frazzled. The more frazzled we become, the more overwhelmed we begin to feel; the more overwhelmed we feel, the more stressed we become. And then we may begin to worry about our increased stress level and the consequences that brings, and the cycle starts all over again.

This cycle begins slowly, sometimes even going unnoticed, but it can gradually begin to grow faster and faster, spinning out of control until something has to give—and, in many cases, that something is our sanity or even our health.

Stress is a vicious cycle! It's like being on a merry-go-round that never stops, leaving you feeling trapped in a blur of colorful horses with wide-eyed, evil looks on their faces. As it spins round and round, you want to jump off, but you are afraid of getting hurt. So even though the horses and the spinning are far from peaceful, you hang on to them for dear life.

You are afraid of what might happen if you jump into the unknown, so you begin to play the "what-if" game, tossing scenarios around in your mind of how to escape and wondering whether the risk will be worth it. But, the longer you ride, the faster it spins and the harder it becomes to find the courage and the willpower to jump. Change seems impossible, then after a while, even though it is uncomfortable and your head is spinning, you get used to the whirling chaos, the frustration, and the worry. And you stop trying to get off all together.

The out-of-control merry-go-round begins to seem normal. And soon it *is* your new normal, and you succumb to living there.

A stressed-out, frazzled life may seem normal to you because it has become so prevalent in our society, but God never told us in his Word that we were helpless to keep stress and chaos from holding our hearts and lives hostage. In fact, he said just the opposite.

We read in John 16:33 that God knew life would be hard, which is why he sent Jesus to us. "I have told you all this so that you may have peace in me. Here on earth you will have many trials and sorrows. But take heart, because I have overcome the world."

Despite what our society wants us to believe, and regardless of the troubles of this world, God's normal is always serenity, and his normal can be our normal, too.

The Search for Serenity

The Serenity Prayer is a common prayer, known to most believers and nonbelievers alike. This prayer was originally a simple, untitled prayer that historically has been dated back as early as 1936 and is credited to a theologian named Reinhold Niebuhr. Niebuhr's prayer goes like this:

> God grant me the serenity to accept the things I cannot change; courage to change the things I can; and wisdom to know the difference.

Sounds easy enough right? I wish I had practiced this art of acceptance when I was stressed to the max from trying to control things I couldn't change. But there is nothing easy about finding serenity, and I know I am not alone in that struggle. Millions of people fall prey to this trap every day and fail to see the difference between what they *can* change and what they *cannot*. Instead of seeking relief from their stress by focusing on the things within their power to change, they spin their wheels, obsessing over problems that are out of their control. As a result, they abandon the possibility of peace, resigning themselves to living in perpetual chaos, simply because they don't believe life can, or should, be different. It's a universal epidemic of abnormal proportions.

Living a life devoid of stress seems so foreign and impossible to most people that they don't even attempt to figure out how to fix the problem; they don't even consider jumping off the spinning merry-go-round. Instead, they surrender to living in the prison of stress that they have come to believe is their fate. Yet it is this surrender to stress that is the primary reason doctors' offices are flooded with scores of patients every day complaining about a myriad of ailments and diseases, unaware that their problems are rooted in stress-related factors. (We'll delve deeper into a discussion of health risks in Chapter Two.)

This serenity prayer epitomizes the idea that the remedy for stress starts in the mind. If we can't change something, there is no need to waste time and energy trying to change it. If we have no power to change a circumstance or person, then every effort to force a change to occur will be futile. And with each futile effort, anxiety builds and stress intensifies.

I came across another rendition of the Serenity Prayer that I liked even more than the first. A philosopher named W. W. Bartley wrote it, and his version goes like this:

> For every ailment under the sun
> There is a remedy, or there is none;
> If there be one, try to find it;
> If there be none, never mind it.

It has the same concept but with a different spin on it—if you can't fix it yourself, never mind it! Put it in God's hands, and let him do the work. To use the old familiar cliché, let go and let God! When we finally surrender to God instead of stress—jump off the merry-go-round with one huge leap of faith—the vicious cycle comes to a screeching halt, and God can finally begin to do his work.

I recently went to the movies with my son to see the feature called *We Bought a Zoo*, starring Matt Damon and Scarlett Johansson. It was a really cute movie to watch, but one thing in particular has stuck in my memory. When Benjamin Mee (Damon) is talking to his son about doing things in life that we are afraid to do, he says to him, "You know, sometimes all you need is twenty seconds of insane courage, just literally twenty seconds of embarrassing bravery. And I promise you, something great will come of it."

Jumping off the merry-go-round of life will take great courage. First, the courage to jump, and, second, the courage to trust that God has something better waiting for you when you land. Being willing to make changes in our lives, and possibly changes within ourselves, definitely takes great courage as well. And even twenty seconds of courage can lead to something great.

If we could change the stress in our lives caused by unpleasant things with the wave of a magic wand, we certainly would; but the reality is that another stressor would surely follow right along behind it. If there is one consistent thing about problems, it would be that they consistently pop up! Stressful events can happen every day. Life is always going to be busy, so trying to find out how life can be completely stress-free would be a pointless and unrewarding journey. This is why it is so important that we learn how to recognize and manage our stress and summon the courage to take a leap of faith towards something greater.

We *can* find peace and joy by learning to control our stress instead of letting it control us. This change will begin to emerge when we focus our energies in the right place and realize that we need to change our attitudes about our stress. Stress typically does not come from the situations in our lives but rather from the ways we handle those situations.

Believe it or not, I came across a third version of the Serenity Prayer that resonated with me even more than the other two. It reads like this:

> God grant me the serenity to accept the people I cannot change,
> the courage to change the only person I can, and the wisdom to
> know that person is me. (author unknown)

True and meaningful change begins from the inside out, and not the other way around. Change has to begin with ourselves, and that takes courage.

The First Step to Freedom

I have witnessed God's power over stress, and I want you to begin putting aside all your typical excuses (including the blame-game tactics). You have complete control over whether you spend life stressed and depressed or happy and fulfilled, despite the circumstances you face.

Still a skeptic? Think your problems are too big and your stress is too overwhelming? Think you have already reached the point of no return? Then my goal is to help you begin to see things from God's perspective—that all things are possible with him—including decreasing your stress.

Once you give in and believe these truths, you can make strides towards freeing your heart and soul from the cultural epidemic of its own, redefined "normal." A normal characterized by chaos brought on by good stressors and bad stressors, but, either way, stress is stress.

Finances. Poor economy. Poverty. Government. Bankruptcy. News headlines. Cancer. Chronic illnesses. Terminal illnesses. Funerals. Abuse. Betrayal. Job loss. Job frustration. Drug or alcohol addiction.

Home foreclosures. Difficult supervisors. Hurtful co-workers. Back stab-bing. Office politics. Divorce. Family problems. Parenting. Teenagers. Housework. Bills. Personal safety. Politics. Marriage. Weddings. New babies. New jobs. New relationships. Old relationships. Crime. Natural disasters. War. Job relocations. Holidays. Birthdays. Death. These are merely a few examples of the good and bad stressors that we face each and every day.

The word "stress" is usually associated with negative or overwhelm-ing circumstances, but there are actually good and bad kinds of stress, some of both of which were mentioned above. But whether we are expe-riencing good stress or bad stress, the physical, emotional, and mental consequences can be the same. Our bodies cannot determine what type of stress we are encountering, just that our emotions are out of whack. So, since stress in every form is here to stay, what we must realize is that it is not the stressful situations in and of themselves that cause our stress but the way we process and handle those stressful situations.

Just because stress is here to stay doesn't mean we are doomed to become its victims. We have the power to fight it by finding courage in God but also by recognizing our body's red flags. We need to live in a state of awareness of what our bodies are trying to tell us.

The worst health consequences of extreme and overwhelming stress begin when basic symptoms are overlooked or when people choose to deliberately ignore their stress, thinking it won't matter. But the reality is that "stress is a major contributing factor either directly or indirectly, to coronary artery disease, cancer, respiratory disorders, accidental injuries, cirrhosis of the liver and suicide; the six leading causes of death in the United States. Stress aggravates other conditions such as multiple sclero-sis, diabetes, herpes, mental illness, alcoholism, drug abuse, and family discord and violence."[1]

When I read that statement, I was shocked. Of course, we have all heard that stress is not good for us, but rarely do we hear that it can actu-ally end life as we know it. Never have I read an obituary in the newspa-per listing the cause of death as "stress." But, because stress is considered normal for our society, people overlook the damage it can cause. They ignore minor health problems until they turn into bigger health problems, often never recognizing that their stress was the actual root cause. However, even those who do recognize the risks continue to stay on the merry-go-round. It's time we all wake up and smell the coffee.

A study conducted by the American Psychological Association (APA) in September and October 2011 stated these findings:

> The annual *Stress in America* survey, which was conducted online by Harris Interactive on behalf of APA among 1,226 U.S. residents in August and September 2011, showed that many Americans consistently report high levels of stress (22 percent reported extreme stress, an 8, 9 or 10 on a 10-point scale where 1 is little or no stress and 10 is a great deal of stress). While reported average stress levels have dipped slightly since the last survey (5.2 on a 10-point scale vs. 5.4 in 2010) many Americans continue to report that their stress has actually increased over time (39 percent report their stress has increased over the past year and 44 percent say their stress has increased over the past 5 years). Yet stress levels exceed people's own definition of what is healthy, with the mean rating for stress of 5.2 on a 10-point scale—1.6 points higher than the stress level Americans reported as healthy.[2]

Simply put, most Americans know they are stressed and that their stress is negatively affecting their health, but they don't have the courage, the willingness, or the knowledge to implement positive changes into their lives.

Based on these survey results, the message is clear: chronic stress has become a public health crisis. In 2010, the APA Chief Executive Officer Norman B. Anderson, PhD, even acknowledged this by saying, "America is at a critical crossroads when it comes to stress and our health."[3]

In November 2010, a stress study showed that 68 percent of people who work are stressed to the point of feeling extremely fatigued and out of control, 64 percent go to work one to four days per year when they are too stressed to be effective, 62 percent take frequent "stress breaks" at work to talk to others, and 44 percent report losing one or more hours per day in productivity because of stress.[4] Although these statistics are mainly employment related, work is only one of the top five stressors, with the other four being personal finances, the economy, child rearing, and relationships.[5]

Despite survey responses from various sources proving that Americans admit that their stress levels are increasing, the vast majority (81 percent) actually believe that they are managing their stress very or somewhat well. Yet the reports of the vast amount of people suffering from physical and emotional symptoms of stress, in addition to seeing negative effects in their relationships, work productivity, and personal lives, would strongly suggest otherwise.[6]

It is believed, based on survey results, that a lack of willpower to change is one of the top challenges for most people: "Americans cite lack of will-power as the biggest barrier to adopting healthier behavior. But 70 percent believe that willpower is something they can learn or improve—if only they had more money, energy or confidence in their ability to change."[7]

Stress is obviously something many people try to ignore, but it is nothing to mess around with, and blaming it all on a lack of willpower is a pretty poor excuse. Willpower comes when there is sufficient infor-mation to signify that a change is crucial. The motivation to change can come from Matthew 19:26, where we are reminded that all things are possible with God.

If you care about your health, your life, your loved ones, your future, and even your walk with Christ, today is the perfect day to admit your need for help. Stop blaming a lack of willpower or blaming other people or living with the mindset that you are at the mercy of your circum-stances. Instead, start by taking a hard look at your mind, spirit, and body, acknowledging any symptoms of stress that you may have been ignoring, and then make a commitment to change with the right motivation.

Admitting our need is one thing; mustering up the initiative to do something about it is quite another. If we do nothing, the consequences could be serious. The world has lots of coping options out there, but if your goal is real change, permanent change, life change, and long-lasting peace—then willpower alone is not going to cut it.

Reflection Questions

1. Have you been habitually blaming people and circumstances for your stress? Make a list of the people or circumstances you have been attributing blame to. Ask God to help you see things from his perspective, and seek his strength to release other people from responsibility for your stress.

2. What Band-Aids have you been using to deal with your stress? Have these Band-Aids been helpful or harmful?

3. How would you finish this statement:

"If_____, I wouldn't be stressed." Write out all of your "if" statements that come to mind.

4. Have the problems you listed above caused you to overlook or discount your blessings? Make a list of blessings that you may have been taking for granted, and spend some time in prayer expressing praise and gratitude to God. Thank God for the difficult circumstances you are in as well, trusting that, in some way, he will use them for his greater purposes.

5. Has stress become your "new normal"? To help clarify this concept, use two columns to do the following. In column one, write out a few descriptive words that signify the "normal" you would like to have (or what used to be normal for you). In column two, write a few words that describe your current normal. Consider the differences, and pray for God to help you see how you can begin making strides to get back to your old normal (for example, responsibilities that you can let go of, stressors you can walk away from, ways to strengthen your faith and find the ability to persevere, people who can support you, etc.).

| | |
| | |

6. Have you ever really asked God for peace and expected to receive it? If yes, reminisce about how you felt when God granted you peace in the midst of a difficult situation. Jot down the emotions and thoughts that come to mind. Then pray and ask God to allow that sweet memory to be fuel for your faith as you face new stressors. If your answer is no, get on your knees today and ask God for this priceless gift of peace and then believe that he will provide it.

7. What can you do today to begin assuming responsibility for your stress?

Stress Busting Scriptures

I have set the LORD always before me.
Because he is at my right hand, I will not be shaken.

Psalm 16:8 NIVp

Cast your cares on the LORD and he will sustain you;
he will never let the righteous fall.

Psalm 55:22 NIV

In my distress I called to the LORD; I called out to my God.
From his temple he heard my voice; my cry came to his ears.

2 Samuel 22:7 NIV

The LORD hears his people when they call to him for help.

He rescues them from all their troubles.

Psalm 34:17

Don't be afraid, for I am with you.
Don't be discouraged, for I am your God.
I will strengthen you and help you.
I will hold you up with my victorious right hand.

Isaiah 41:10

Chapter Two

Does It Really Matter?

If stress is so prevalent in our world today, should we even attempt to fight it? Is it something that deserves our undivided attention, or is it simply just a sign of the times that we should accept and live with?

Even though stress might be the new normal for our culture, it is not the normal that God ever intended for us. In a recent article in *USA Today*, an interesting shift in stress statistics was attributed to a paradigm shift in perceptions about stress. This article, based on results from the APA survey that, I mentioned in Chapter One (39 percent said their stress rose last year, 17 percent said it dropped, 44 percent said it stayed the same), stated that although the amount of people saying they were stressed had decreased, it didn't mean that people were no longer feeling as stressed.[8]

So if that is the case, why did the overall stress percentage decline? The article went on to explain that the economic climate, money, and other cultural stressful issues have not changed. So the decline in reported stress is likely because stress has become the new normal for life and people have been under so much stress in the past few years that they have simply adapted to it.[9]

Stress is like a ticking time bomb and, if ignored, will eventually result in an emotional implosion—riddling our spirits with virtual bullet holes, destroying our bodies, which are to be God's temples, and scattering emotional shrapnel over every area of our lives. Even though people have learned to adapt to stress as a normal part of life, our bodies are not quite so cooperative.

The damage that stress can have is without limitation, and continuing to ignore stress not only causes an onslaught of physical problems but it also serves as proof that we have not been caring for our bodies as God intended. Even stress eating and stress caused by the consequences of overeating are further evidence of neglecting our duties as caretakers.

One Wednesday evening I was driving my then sixteen-year-old daughter Morgan to church, and she expressed that she was hungry (which was nothing new). But since I knew it would be a while before we returned home. I pulled through a fast-food drive-through window to get her a quick bite. She immediately ordered a Double Baconator Combo—you probably know which meal I'm talking about . . . the huge hamburger with two thick patties, six strips of bacon, cheese, and all the toppings, plus an oversized fry and a large soft drink. I could never eat a hamburger that big and was amazed that, with her 110-pound self, she thought she could. I just assumed that her eyes were bigger than her stomach.

As she dove into the bag, reaching for her hot, delicious-smelling meal, I gently warned her, in my most concerned and loving mom voice, that bad eating habits and fatty foods would eventually catch up to her from a weight perspective, but, more importantly, they were very unhealthy. Then our conversation took an interesting twist.

The week before this trip to church, I had been studying the book of Leviticus, which focuses on the building of God's temple by the Israelites after they had left Egypt, and, apparently, I had "temple on the brain" syndrome.

As I continued driving, I urged Morgan to remember that her body was God's temple; therefore, she should take care of it, and part of taking care of our bodies is eating healthy. She had no choice but to listen to my well-meaning lecture since she was trapped in the car with me, and eventually she replied (while wearing that typical teenage facial expression of utter confusion at the parental wisdom she was being given), "Mom, are you trying to tell me that eating this hamburger is a sin?!"

I laughed, and our comical conversation went on for several more minutes as I attempted to convince her of the importance of treating her body as God's temple, and she simultaneously continued to hold her ground, arguing that eating that hamburger was not a sin.

It wasn't that I had anything against hamburgers, but, after having read countless details about the Tabernacle (the tent version of the Temple), I had embraced a newfound appreciation for its sacredness and was encouraged by knowing that the Lord actually resided in the Temple in biblical times. I admired the hours of work that were devoted to building the Tabernacle and the many rules and requirements that God set forth regarding honoring and caring for it.

In the New Testament, we are reminded many times about how we are now God's dwelling place, instead of a tent or building made by the hands of men. We no longer have to worship, pray, or converse with God in a specific designated place, because his Spirit lives within us. We can talk to him anytime we want, regardless of where we are. So for those who have accepted Jesus Christ as their Savior and who believe in the Father, Son, and Holy Ghost, we are indeed his holy temple.

First Corinthians 3:16–17 says, "Don't you know that you yourselves are God's temple and that God's Spirit lives in you? If anyone destroys God's temple, God will destroy him; for God's temple is sacred, and you are that temple" (NIV).

At first glance, the verses above seem to imply an overwhelming responsibility to understand that we truly are God's temple, that we are the only ones who can take care of it, and that he has commanded us to do just that. But, most importantly, he warns us that there are consequences for ignoring this command—consequences that could potentially lead to destruction.

Healthy eating is not the only way to care for our bodies, but it is an important issue that is often ignored by many. Unfortunately, the society we live in has become accustomed to and even expectant of larger portions, resulting in overeating and the daily consumption of unhealthy, overprocessed, fattening foods, which has led to record numbers of obesity in America. A recent article in the *New York Times* stated that "nearly 34 percent of adults are obese, more than double the percentage 30 years ago. The share of obese children tripled during that time, to 17 percent." It also stated that, according to the Centers for Disease Control and Prevention, Americans might have reached their peak of obesity.[10]

I found it interesting that statistics on stress show that stress has increased and statistics on obesity show that obesity has increased. I feel confident there is a connection. Although there are many other factors that often play a role in overeating, how a person feels is going to drive their behaviors; and, for many people, eating is a way to cope with stress.

It's easy to see how this could happen. After all, babies quickly learn that eating makes them feel safe and loved; God created us to hunger for those sweet emotions. As adults, we still long to have those same emotional needs met, but that longing can turn into trouble if we try to meet those needs with food. When overeating becomes our only way to cope, weight gain is imminent, frustration and self-condemnation kick in, and stress is sure to have yet another excuse to intrude on our lives. Some people may be completely unaware that food has become a stress relief mechanism for them, while others know they have a problem but feel helpless to fix it.

"Survey findings also show that many people who suffer from depression and obesity say they are unable to take the necessary steps to reduce their stress and therefore engage in unhealthy behaviors. People living with depression or obesity report significantly higher average stress levels . . . than the rest of the population."[11]

The term "vicious cycle" comes back to mind. There are steps that depressed or obese individuals can take to tackle any further symptoms of stress, such as eating healthy snacks throughout the day instead of three large meals, regulating portion sizes, avoiding too much caffeine, and making time for regular exercise. Although these seem like commonsense solutions, sometimes the vicious cycle of stress keeps suffering people from taking the needed steps to begin making strides for better mental and physical health.

In fact, studies show that those struggling with depression or obesity are significantly more likely to say they do not think they are doing enough to manage their stress.[12] They know the problem exists but lack the knowledge, willpower, or motivation to address the problems or seek out resolutions.

Poor choices usually lead to more poor choices, and all poor choices lead to stress. Unhealthy eating is a serious epidemic in our country, but unhealthy living is just as prevalent, and, frankly, just as dangerous. Therefore, finding the motivation to overcome our stress has become more important than ever before.

Living a life plagued by the disease of stress and busyness is not only unhealthy living, bringing with it the potential for serious negative consequences to our physical bodies, but it also carries a looming threat to our hearts and souls as well. Understanding the importance that God places on caring for his temple, our bodies, cannot be overlooked as we begin this journey to discover a "stressed-less life."

It matters to God whether you are stressed, because he knows that stress puts your body, his temple, in great jeopardy. I hope that by the end of this book you will see why it should matter to you, too.

Recognizing Your Personal Stressors

Stress doesn't happen overnight. Though an unexpected or tragic situation can spontaneously rage into our lives, causing immediate stress and worry, it normally takes a period of time for stress to reach its full potential. Any situation or circumstance, either good or bad, can cause stress; so, the importance of figuring out what stresses us most is a key factor in the mission towards a peace-filled life—bringing us one step closer to getting a taste of the sweet joy-filled life that we crave.

In the same way that a doctor cannot prescribe a treatment for your illness until he knows what the illness is, we cannot address our own struggle with stress until we know what is actually causing the problem.

The stress itself does not need to be the focus, because that is merely the external manifestation of the internal problem. Instead, we need to identify the cause of the stress by doing an in-depth self-assessment of our raw emotions. In many cases, our stress is coming from something that seems to be part of our normal, so we overlook the toll it takes on us.

For example, we may not realize that every time we have to deal with a certain person, our blood pressure rises and our heart races. We may not realize that a particular task at work causes us to feel anxious and overwhelmed. We may not realize that we are subconsciously worrying about a situation that we thought we had under control. This has happened to me occasionally, when I didn't realize how stressed I was over something until my stomach began having serious issues. Only when the external symptom showed up did I realize the internal anxiety I had been harboring.

Determining your stressors takes a personal commitment to being in tune with your body and feelings, because what is stressful for another person may not be stressful for you at all, and vice versa. Case in point, some people love to speak in front of groups, while others turn pale faced and get weak in the knees just thinking about it. Some people enjoy working under deadlines and are more productive when pressured, while others may get so tense under pressure that they can't even think straight. Some people love to spend time with family members, while others would rather have their toes stomped on repeatedly with six inch, red high heels than go to a family gathering. Some people know just what to say when someone is hurting, while others are at a loss for words and break out in a cold sweat during the awkward silence. Some people value change and can always roll with the punches, while others may become mentally paralyzed when change is on the way.

God made each of us unique. Therefore, no two people are alike in their feelings. And as a result, no two people will ever experience, endure, or manage stress the same way. Along these same lines, it is also important to know whether you are more vulnerable to stress than other people, and this answer lies in your personality type. For example, people who are high strung, impatient, and ambitious, may be more at risk for anxiety and experiencing stress-related physical problems. Why? Because they will probably push themselves to the breaking point to accomplish their goals at all costs. On the other hand, someone who is more laid back and passive may not get stressed at all, even when faced with the possibility of falling short of meeting his or her expectations, or those of someone else.

A couple of other things to consider are that there are certain occupations that may be more stressful than others. And sometimes family history can play a role in determining a person's ability to handle stress, such as if there are any mental illnesses in the family, a history of depression, or if the person grew up in a household that was in a constant state of stress, resulting in the mind being trained to be on stress alert and on guard all the time.

But regardless of your personality, occupation, family history, or whether you are more prone to stress than the next person, the fact remains that too much stress can be dangerous, and the damage of stress does not play favorites.

Self-Assessment

Before we go any further, I want you to take this opportunity to begin thinking about the major stressors in your life. In order to embark on the journey of turning our stressors over to God and letting him replace them with peace, we must first figure out exactly what those stressors really are.

I encourage you to take a few moments and fill out the following table. Think about all the people, problems, and circumstances in your life that are causing you stress right now. But don't get stressed while you are thinking about them!

Although this self-assessment / life examination may not be a fun task, it is necessary if you seriously desire to overcome your stress and begin to heal. You may think you already know what your biggest stressors are, but the possibility exists that some problems and harmful emotions have been festering just under the surface. And God is ready to walk alongside you to dig them all up.

Pray before you begin. Ask God to open your eyes to issues that you may not have thought of before. Ask him to help you see things in a new perspective and for this exercise to truly be one that will jump-start you on the road to stress recovery.

Once you are done, follow the instructions in the paragraph after the assessment.

Personal Stress Self-Assessment

The Problem	How Does This Problem Make You Feel?	How Is the Problem Affecting Your Life?	Do You Have Control or Power to Change This Problem?
Adult son continuing to make the same mistakes & moving back home + to thinking he's the cause of them	Overwhelmed - Anxious, panicky tension, upset disappointed - scared - resentful - ashamed, hurt - nervous	On edge - headache - palpitations - agitated - short-tempered - mad - vengeful ugly - sad	NO
High credit card balance	out of control angry - not in control of the spending anxious-worried	Anxiety, nervous worried, scared, unorganized	Yes
School	overwhelmed anxious, nervous tense, headaches	Headaches - Can't think straight - insomnia - intense dreams of homework	yes
no close friends	Abandoned - Resentful - Alone - Discouraged unloved	makes me withdrawn Afraid to get close to people Sad, lonely	yes NO

Unorganized messy house	Overwhelmed Stressed - tense - disorganized sloppy	mind racing upset - angry - mad - giving - up	yes / NO
Daughters wedding	excited - nervous - anxious - unsure of ideas - imperfect	anxious - overwhelmed uneasy roller coaster	NO / yes
not spiritual enough	Bad person, neglectful, sinner, not changing	never getting over my answered, stress' disappoint discouraged	yes
Gratification shopping	good then bad like mad then anxious and nervous	Bills left give up. wasted money on forbidden clothes	yes
Relatives parents - siblings	abandoned - stressed - anxious - angry - upset vengeful hateful	Bothersome mind reeling old memories pent up anger - resentment Constant stress	NO

Now, take a look at your list. Pause and pray over each and every one of the issues that you listed above. Be sure you answered honestly about whether you have any control over the problem. If you do not, admit whether you have been trying to fix or control the outcome on your own. Ask God to grant you the courage and strength to let those problems go, and let him take over. If other problems come to mind later, come back to this page and jot them down as well so you will have a record of everything you are turning over to God.

Close this reflection activity by praying the prayer below or by pouring your heart out to God in your own words.

Dear heavenly Father, I know you are sovereign and almighty, and I ask for your hand to be upon my life. I am in much need of your strength, wisdom, discernment, and courage to help me deal with these difficult situations or people in my life. I need your guidance and I desire to lay these burdens at your feet. Give me the strength to do so. Please pour your grace and mercy all over my soul, and lift these pressures from my heart. Help me to seek out your ways and your desires each morning when I awake, instead of trudging through my days in the same manner that I have always done. I pray for your supernatural intervention in my life and in my heart. Equip me with perseverance in my quest to fully trust in you with all of my problems. Please fill my heart with a peace that surpasses all understanding, and lead me into a closer relationship with you as I progress through this book. In Jesus' name I pray, Amen.

Learning how to manage and deal with the stressful situations in our lives sets us in motion to discover a life of peace and joy, and Jesus holds the key to unlocking the secret of a less stressed life. Let's prepare our hearts to be transformed by a holy God, as we begin to expose the truth about the destruction that can come upon us by choosing to ignore the obvious and not treating our bodies as God's temple.

A Matter of Life and Death

While employed at the accounting firm I have already told you about, I not only experienced stress, I experienced the destructive consequences of full-blown stress sickness. Although it appeared to be a great career with a successful organization, it demanded a high tolerance for unrelenting stress.

The hour-long commute, the deadlines, the rampant office politics, the demanding and demeaning boss, the cutthroat tactics, the workload, the worry, the overtime, the frustration, the travel, added onto three small children, married life, maintaining house and home, and extended family concerns, all worked together to turn me into one overwhelmed, overcommitted, overstressed, overfrazzled, burnt-out young woman.

As I've made clear already, I knew deep in my heart that something was wrong, but, since everyone in the firm lived and worked under the same amount of stress, I honestly thought it was normal. However, my opinion gradually changed as I grasped the realization that I was not only miserable and unhappy but I had started to experience more than my fair share of unexpected, unexplained, and bothersome health issues.

For a girl in her thirties, I was the picture of health. I had no idea that my out-of-control stress level was taking a huge physical toll on me in every way possible.

The first of many issues that began to plague my body was consistent blurry vision, which prompted me to visit the eye doctor. I had always been blessed with excellent eyesight and had never worn glasses or contacts, so this strange and rather sudden issue with my vision was highly unusual. I was sure that I needed bifocals at an early age, but even after repeated visits, the optometrist continued to assure me that my vision was near perfect. In my frustration, I pondered the possibility that maybe my chosen optometrist had finished last in his graduating class, since he was continually unable to diagnose my obvious onset of partial blindness.

The second problem was a little more serious. Because of ongoing heart palpitations, I contacted a cardiologist, who performed EKG tests, various blood work, and a couple of heart ultrasounds. I even wore a heart monitor for a few weeks in an attempt to catch my unusual heart activity on tape, and I felt sure that I was a prime candidate to keel over of a heart attack at my desk any day. The irregular heartbeats and unusually hard pounding in my chest, sometimes hard enough to wake me from a deep sleep in the middle of the night, scared me immensely. After all, I was Mommy to three little children who needed me and wife to a husband I loved. I couldn't bear the thought of something happening to me, and so my worry was compounded even more. Plus, I didn't want to die.

I was also concerned at my inability to ever take a good, deep breath. It seemed my lungs always felt restricted, as if a fifty-pound boulder had taken up residence on my chest. But, just like the optometrist, the cardiologist could find nothing medically wrong with my heart or my lungs.

If those issues weren't bad enough, I began suffering from severe gastrointestinal problems, including constant diarrhea, stomach cramps, and irregular bathroom habits, thus landing me at the gastroenterologist and the colon doctor. A stomach ulcer was suspected but not found, and all other tests came back void as well. So it was concluded I could possibly have irritable bowel syndrome (IBS), primarily from the inability to find anything else wrong. I was given a weak prescription and some generic suggestions on how to manage my issues through diet.

Stupid doctors. My cynicism and frustration were convincing me that all my doctors obviously had finished last in their class.

To make matters worse, I was practically overdosing on acetaminophen every day as I tried to manage my chronic headaches. I even began to wonder whether I should invest in the stocks of some of the pharmaceutical companies to at least justify the money I was giving them every week. I also wondered whether taking such a large volume of over-the-counter medications was what was causing me to be so forgetful. And I won't even go into my pathetic sleep habits, how every night I slept like a baby . . . with colic.

Despite my attempts for more than a year to find something, anything, medically wrong with me, the doctors could find no physical evidence of any serious medical concern. I know it sounds like I was just a crazy hypochondriac looking for problems that weren't there, but, you see, it wasn't that I wanted something to be wrong with me—no one hopes to have medical problems.

What I wanted, what I was desperately seeking, what my heart yearned for, was a prescription for peace. I was completely unaware that all of my external problems, which made me feel like my body was falling apart, were merely symptoms of the internal spiritual problems that no doctor had the wisdom to diagnose.

I wanted someone to help me find a solution for the chaos that raged within me, but, since no concrete answers could be found, my physical health continued to decline. I wanted to feel better again. I just wanted my life back. I wanted peace. I wanted joy. I wanted to be happy. But when answers evaded doctors and relief never came, I conceded that change was hopeless. I just needed to accept that these health nuisances were a new part of my life, put on my big girl panties, and learn to live with them. They had become part of my new norm. So I surrendered to my fate—a life filled with overwhelming stress—and decided I needed to stand up and take it like a man . . . I mean, a woman.

All that time, I was clueless that my out-of-control stress level was the culprit of all of my health problems, from the smallest ones to the biggest. I was unaware that I was bringing destruction upon my own body as 1 Corinthians 3 warns us about. Yet what was worse than overlooking the toll that my stress was taking on my body was overlooking the toll it was taking on my heart. And to be perfectly honest, I didn't even know what real peace looked like.

What Peace Is to You

When most people think of Jesus, with the exception of when he was hanging on the cross, they usually visualize him as a peaceful person living a peaceful life. Thanks to infinite paintings dating back hundreds of years depicting Jesus as a soft-hearted, gentle-looking, bearded man, it is easy to falsely believe he never really had to deal with stress. These paintings often show portrayals of God's Son in a headshot drawing, while quietly gazing off with a serene look on his face or praying peacefully to the heavens on bended knee with his hands folded across his chest or sitting happily under a tree with smiling children perched on his lap.

Although Jesus is the Prince of Peace, always has been and always will be, his life was a far cry from being stress-free. Obviously, the crucifixion was the most stressful day in his life, but he actually experienced and dealt with unrelenting stress each and every day until his earthly life ended and he ascended into Heaven to sit at the right hand of his Father.

The biggest difference between the stress that Jesus faced and the stress that we face is only that he was better equipped to handle it. The fact that he was sinless and pure certainly helped with his reactions, but he still had to manage the human emotions that were present in his human form. The shortest verse in the Bible is John 11:35: "Jesus wept." These two words alone prove that Jesus felt strong emotion and stress was a part of his life. His words and actions speak volumes for how we can handle the stress in our own lives, through the strength and wisdom that he willingly offers. Jesus did nothing in sin to cause his stress and did nothing in response to stress to compound his stress, because he knew full well what it meant to have peace despite stressful circumstances.

If you think about it, there are different ways to define peace, and each one of us may choose any one of those variations. For example, peace to a mom of several young toddlers might be a lack of noise. Peace to a busy employee would be a day without problems or deadlines. Peace to a high school student might be the absence of a bully who taunts him or her every day. Peace to a person struggling financially would mean knowing that all of the bills are paid.

Peace means different things to different people in different seasons of life. How we define peace, and where we are looking to find that peace, is the only common denominator we have with our sweet Jesus.

Many people think that the definition of peace is simply the absence of conflict, but the absence of conflict is only a temporary situation that will eventually come to a close. It is a fragile view of peace, because the peace desired is based solely on one's circumstances.

A much better definition of peace is one that rests on the ability to rise above our circumstances, overcome our innate tendency to stress out over problems, and learn to remain calm and confident despite what is going on around us. That is real peace—a peace based on Christ, not on people or circumstances. A peace based on faith, not on personal desires being met. A peace based on a quieted heart, not on a quiet house. A peace based on the love of Jesus, not on an easy day at work. A peace based on trusting God in all things, not just the easy things we can handle with no problem.

A peace that is present in our hearts, even when our entire life is over-flowing with chaos. That is the kind of peace only Jesus can give, and, once we get a taste of that kind of peace, we are never the same again.

✍ Reflection Questions

1. Do you feel like a ticking time bomb? What situations are causing you to feel that way today? *Yes - not getting things accomplished with my son - him not being motivated to get his life back on track to get further ahead. Not having my wedding dress picked out. Not sure on my classes. Not having my loan yet to pay credit cards.*

2. What changes could you implement in your life to begin taking better care of yourself, God's temple? Consider inviting a friend to join you in your journey to live healthier and less stressed. Share your personal commitments for change so you can hold each other accountable and offer support and encouragement to meet your goals. *Exercising everyday, changing my eating habits. Doing relaxation everyday. Praying more - reading my spiritual books. Detoxifying my body.*

3. What are some of your biggest personal stressors? In what ways can you prepare in advance to avoid getting upset by them in the future? *Pressing my myself to get things done now - rushing through everything I do. Rethinking and analyzing everything.*
- Taking time to enjoy the moment
- Slowing down
- Re-organizing & not wasting time on trivial things (consumation of going over the same material or things)

4. Have you been experiencing any physical problems that could be rooted in stress? If so, list them below. *Anxiety, tension, headaches, palpitations, TMJ, insomia, IBS, sour stomach, Body aches + twitches, restless legs, racing heart ready to explode*

5. If you listed some symptoms above, ask yourself whether you have been ignoring them or possibly attributing them to something other than stress-related factors. *Some are attributed to Bad eating habits and non exeruse To much caffeine*

6. Consider whether any of your symptoms could be endangering your overall health. Are there any changes that need to be made in your life so that stress doesn't damage your long-term health and life span? *Yes - Need to let things go - Stop dwelling on the past - give everything over to God - stop trying to control everything - Deep breathing -*

7. Is it possible that your stress has created a barrier between you and God? If your answer is yes, have a conversation with God about it, and write out your prayer below, or consider praying this prayer:

Dear Lord, I never realized that ignoring my stress signified that I didn't care about my body, your temple. I simply never considered the fact that my stress could take such a huge toll on me physically. Ashamedly, I also never recognized the toll it was taking on me spiritually. I ask for your forgiveness for allowing my stressful circumstances to pull me away from you, instead of pushing me toward you. I am beginning to see that, though I have been blinded to it until now, stress is a bigger problem in my life than I once thought. Jesus, please fill me with peace and assurance that you are with me, even though I have abandoned you and even though I have felt abandoned by you at times. Forgive my doubting heart.

Help me to remember that you never leave or forsake your children and that I can trust that you are always with me. Empower me through your Spirit to take a stand for my health, my family, my future, and my faith and to persevere in whatever it takes to gain control of my life again. Walk beside me as I embark on this journey to be less stressed and as I open my spiritual eyes to see and feel you at work, especially on the hardest of days. In Jesus name, Amen.

Stress Busting Scriptures

My son, pay attention to what I say; listen closely to my words. Do not let them out of your sight, keep them within your heart; for they are life to those who find them and health to a man's whole body.

Proverbs 4:20–22 NIV

✍

Then they cried to the LORD in their trouble, and he saved them from their distress. He sent forth his word and healed them; he rescued them from the grave. Let them give thanks to the LORD for his unfailing love and his wonderful deeds for men.

Psalm 107:19–21 NIV

✍

"So don't worry about these things, saying, 'What will we eat? What will we drink? What will we wear?' These things dominate the thoughts of unbelievers, but your heavenly Father already knows all your needs. Seek the Kingdom of God above all else, and live righteously, and he will give you everything you need. "So don't worry about tomorrow, for tomorrow will bring its own worries. Today's trouble is enough for today."

Matthew 6:31–34

✍

"I am leaving you with a gift—peace of mind and heart. And the peace I give is a gift the world cannot give. So don't be troubled or afraid."

John 14:27

✍

"I have told you all this so that you may have peace in me. Here on earth you will have many trials and sorrows. But take heart, because I have overcome the world."

John 16:33

Chapter Three

The Silent Killer

No doubt about it—stress can kill. If it doesn't kill us, it will absolutely leave its mark. Another study I came across recently shared a few more interesting facts about stress findings:

- Seventy-five percent of the general population experiences at least "some stress" every two weeks (National Health Interview Survey).
- Half of those experience moderate or high levels of stress during the same two-week period.
- Millions of Americans suffer from unhealthy levels of stress at work. (A study several years ago estimated the number to be eleven million—given events since that time, this number has certainly more than tripled.)
- Worker's compensation claims for "mental stress" in California rose 200–700 percent in the 1980s (whereas all other causes remained stable or declined).
- Stress contributes to heart disease, high blood pressure, strokes, and other illnesses in many individuals.

- Stress also affects the immune system, which protects us from many serious diseases.
- Tranquilizers, antidepressants, and antianxiety medications account for one-fourth of all prescriptions written in the U.S. each year.
- Stress also contributes to the development of alcoholism, obesity, suicide, drug addiction, cigarette addiction, and other harmful behaviors.
- The U.S. Public Health Service has made reducing stress by the year 2000 one of its major health promotion goals.[13]

That last tidbit of information jumped off the page when I first read it, where it says that the U.S. Public Health Service had made stress reduction a high priority goal because it knew the toll it was reaping on our population as a whole.

Stress is a chronic disease that is rampant in today's society, so much more so than it was even when the statement above was made over twelve years ago. If the Public Health Service acknowledges the problem, why do we accept stress as normal and ignore its consequences? Consider this: If you found out you had cancer, would you refuse treatment that might save your life? Of course not! Likewise, if you know you are stressed to an unhealthy level yet refuse to discover the real problems and implement necessary changes to help eliminate or reduce your stress, then you are, in essence, refusing treatment and jeopardizing your life.

Most emotional and physical symptoms of stress and depression are not typically caused by the circumstances themselves, but instead by how our minds perceive what is going on and how our hearts hold up under the pressure. We have seen the physical effects that stress can have on our lives, now let's take a look at the havoc it can reap on our mental capacities.

Mind over Matter

Women are becoming victims of stress even more than men, primarily because of stress over the economy and finances. Currently there are six million women who are struggling with depression. Not that stress is the only factor that causes depression, but there is a proven link.

A doctor from the Mayo Clinic wrote an online article about how chronic stress can increase the risk of developing depression, especially for people who do not use the proper coping methods or acknowledge their need for stress reduction. He confirmed that stress itself isn't abnormal, but the way we deal with stress can undermine our long-term health. If left unmanaged, chronic stress can lead to frequent bad moods, strained relationships, and possibly even the inability to carry out normal daily routines—all of which can begin a dangerous downward spiral towards clinical depression.[14]

So friend, do you still think stress doesn't matter? I know some of these statistics and reference materials are a lot to take in, but I hope they have opened your eyes to the physical and mental risks that you are taking when you choose to ignore your stress. It's time you get off the merry-go-round and take back your life before it's too late.

Discovering the Great Physician

It pains me to think of the number of times I needed the healing of God's powerful hands but instead sought out attention from doctors or tried to rid myself of issues through self-diagnoses, medications, and sleep. What a shame that when we find ourselves in the most desperate of situations, we are too stubborn to ask God for healing until we get to that "end-of-our-rope" stage. Granted, there are times when we need to seek out medical advice, but there are also times when we need to seek out holy intervention instead.

God is often referred to as "the Great Physician," but typically when people use this term, they are praying for physical healing for a loved one or for themselves. Although praying for physical healing is important and necessary, we already know that Jesus walked the earth to provide something even more important than physical healing. He came bringing spiritual healing that not only saves the soul but saturates it with peace and minimizes the stress in our hearts.

I love the way Psalm 103:2–5 reminds us of this saving grace: "Let all that I am praise the LORD; may I never forget the good things he does for me. He forgives all my sins and heals all my diseases. He redeems me from death and crowns me with love and tender mercies. He fills my life with good things. My youth is renewed like the eagle's!"

The reason Christ came to earth was because we needed him, now and eternally. God knew we would one day find ourselves in a pit, whether deep or shallow, and that we would all need to be redeemed by his love and renewed in our spirits. God also knew just how much we needed a Great Physician, and out of compassion for us he sent his Son Jesus to fill that role. In order to tap into his healing power and find peace, we simply have to seek him first—above all else. Above practical strategies and tips for stress management. Above lengthy yoga sessions. Above breathing and relaxation exercises. Above shopping therapy. Above bubble baths. Above all else.

Unfortunately, our typical way of handling stress is not to put God above all else. In fact, it seems that sometimes we tend to view God like the Red Cross—someone to call upon when we are in grave, unexpected, or seemingly hopeless crisis situations. We often see him as someone to look to for help, only when we have exhausted all other options. However, God's desire is to be a part of our lives in the good and bad times, when we are stressed and when we are not. He wants to be our first responder, not our last resort, and he came to heal those who are sick in heart, not just sick in body.

A few years ago, I experienced a very stressful situation in my personal life. After exhausting every other option to deal with my problem, I found myself pleading for God's intervention. It was a very emotionally demanding situation, one where I had been betrayed and hurt and felt devastated by the actions of someone that I had trusted. When this betrayal came to light, my emotions were all-consuming, and the awareness of overwhelming stress had rammed into my heart with the force of a fast-moving freight train.

I prayed and prayed and prayed some more. I cried and cried and cried some more. As I cried and prayed, I asked God for peace that I thought was impossible to grasp. I wondered whether I could ever feel it again, considering this emotional tragedy that I was going through. I prayed for the hurt to go away. I prayed for the anger at this person to minimize. I prayed for the ability to forgive, even though I felt it was not deserved. I prayed for a miracle to happen in me, and for me. I needed God to heal the broken pieces of my heart, weaving a soft thread of his scarlet peace through the frayed edges of my life. And in a matter of days after seeking his intervention, I noticed a change. I felt a sense of peace and serenity that I could not explain. At one point, I realized that I had not focused on that devastating problem for several hours because it was no longer at the forefront of my thoughts. As a result, I was feeling joyful, despite this less-than-joyful circumstance that I was going through.

But, I thought to myself, *how could this be? How can I feel joyful and full of peace when this devastating situation is still raging through my life like an F4 tornado?*

For a moment I felt confused, wondering, *Why am I so calm? Why am I not obsessing about that problem every second? Why am I not more distraught and worried? Why do I not feel that burning anger in my heart anymore? How is it possible that I am feeling happy in the middle of this terrible storm in my life?* It surpassed my understanding.

Then God quickened my heart and reminded me that just a few days earlier I had turned that problem over to him. I had asked him to intervene and to fill me with a peace that surpassed my understanding. I had begged for joy amid this joyless time. I had asked, and he had given.

God heard that prayer of anxiousness and desperation. He heard my loud pleading for peace, and he answered. He had dried my tears and lifted that weight off of my shoulders. He was now carrying my cross, and I no longer had to. I had sought out a cure from the Great Physician, and he had provided it. Not a cure for the problem but a cure for my heart as I dealt with the problem in his strength and under the refuge of his love.

I want to see you discover that feeling of hope that can be achieved once you realize that a stressful life is not normal and definitely not worth the costs. I want you to begin to believe that you can have a peace that surpasses your understanding, regardless of what is going in your life, just as we are promised in Philippians 4:7, which says, "Then you will experience God's peace, which exceeds anything we can understand. His peace will guard your hearts and minds as you live in Christ Jesus."

I want to help you step out of your stress zone and into the faith zone where you really belong and where peace flows like a river. Where Christ is waiting patiently for you to call out to him so he can pour his peace into your life. My heart longs for Christ to use this book to lead you into a place of serenity that can only be found through a relationship with him.

We can't always remove ourselves from problem situations—quit stressful jobs, walk away from responsibilities, turn from difficult relationships, or simply wish things away—which is exactly why it is so important for faithful Christians to believe that managing our stress begins with Christ, instead of empty techniques and strategies that the enemy tries to deceive us with.

We need his strength, guidance, peace, and joy more than we will ever know, and, the longer we continue to ignore the problem, the more destruction this silent killer will cause. Unfortunately, millions of people will keep on doing what they have always done, even if it's detrimental to their health and their future, simply because everybody else is doing it and because society has accepted stress as the norm and adapted to it. Even though swimming against the current takes more effort and dedication than following the crowd, it will always pay off in the long run.

Swimming against the Current

Parenting and child rearing are among the top five stressors of the general population, and I can understand why. There are days when I feel like the stress of being a parent just might be the death of me, and other days when I absolutely can't get enough of my sweet children. But despite my larger-than-life love for them, sometimes the thought of a minivacation from parenting (if there were such a thing) sounds mighty enticing, especially on the days when I am suffering from a severe case of parental exhaustion.

When children are little, the demands they place on a parent are physically exhausting, to say the least. But, as they grow into adolescents, the physical exhaustion is quickly replaced by emotional exhaustion in its highest form.

Instead of our bodies suffering through sleepless nights and the constant smell of poopy diapers, our hearts suffer with worry over whether our children will make it home safely and whether they are strong enough to stand up for what is right in the face of peer pressure. In fact, despite all my stressful experiences in life, I honestly don't think I knew what real stress was until I was faced with the daunting task of raising teenagers.

Trying to raise up godly children in an ungodly world can be draining. There is so much stuff to deal with every day that we pour ourselves out and sometimes end up feeling empty and discouraged. What is stuff, you ask? Let me throw out a few examples of some of the more minor "stuff" in our house:

- time-consuming homework, which sometimes results in frustrated outbursts and refusal to complete, followed by punishments for a bad attitude about doing said homework
- anxiety, and sometimes tears, over not understanding math, which is worsened by parental inability to help because somehow adding and subtracting are now much more complicated than they were thirty years ago
- teen drama; girl drama; mean-girl drama; and more drama
- cheers and tears over boyfriends and girlfriends
- spending too much time on Facebook, Twitter, Instagram, and Pinterest, resulting in computer or phone privileges becoming restricted
- trying to make new friends, keep old friends, and fit in with all friends

- fashion choices that are nixed because of either being border-line immodest, or just plain unattractive
- unfair coaches, unfair teachers, unfair grades, and unfair rules

And let's take a peek at some of the more major "stuff" topics:

- "Everybody else gets to watch that reality show, why can't I?"
- "Everybody else can stay out until 2:00 A.M. after the concert!"
- "Everybody else gets to go to the party, why can't I go?"
- "My friends' parents don't even care what they do. Why can't you be more like them?"
- "Everybody else I know doesn't even have a curfew."
- "Everybody else gets to stay up until 11:00 P.M. on school nights!"
- "What's wrong with wanting to go out with my friends every single night of the week?"
- "Everybody does it, Mom; it's just what kids do these days" (regardless of what "it" is).
- "Everybody else gets to text all night long. What difference does it make?"
- "Everybody else gets to play video games for six hours. Why can't I do it?"

I'll stop there—you get the picture. *Everybody else* seems to be allowed to do *everything*! Of course, I don't really believe that *everybody else* is getting to do all the *everythings* they want. But there are certainly days when it honestly seems that way, even to me. Days when, if the words "everybody else" are spoken one more time, they could potentially cause a very ugly mommy meltdown.

Maybe you can relate, because you too have had your fill of the "everybody else" card being dealt. In fact, you may even feel like you are swimming upstream against a rapid, powerful current of hands-off parenting that seems to be a growing trend in our society. It is easy to see why that style of parenting is becoming so popular—it appears less stressful.

After all, who doesn't want to avoid hostile arguments, enforcing curfews, implementing discipline, and doling out punishments? Who wouldn't want to quit the full-time job of monitoring whereabouts, tracking activity, and approving friend choices? The temptation for parents to go along with what "everybody else" is doing, especially if it means keeping some shred of peace in the household, is sometimes stronger than the strength to persevere through the most stressful parenting years. However, the one thing that sets Christian parents apart from the rest of the world is the willingness to faithfully persevere in their parenting values, no matter how stressful the journey becomes and no matter how unpopular it makes them.

Christian parents are called to be in the world but not of the world and to be set apart for their children's sake—not set aside by their children when they reach the age of fourteen. Instead of allowing the stress of parenting to tempt us to throw in the towel, we need to throw ourselves on our knees every day, praying for their safety and their decision making and asking God to get a good, strong grasp on their hearts before something or someone else does.

Proverbs 22:6, a popular verse on the topic of parenting, says, "Train a child in the way he should go, and when he is old he will not turn from it" (NIV). Training a child up in the way he or she should go does not stop when we leave the sanctuary. It is a call to pursue God's ways every day with unwavering determination and unending perseverance and learning to manage the never-ending onslaught of "stuff" without giving up. There will always be cases when even the best efforts to raise a child with a solid foundation of faith may seem futile when that child appears to be rejecting God's teaching or choosing paths that are not good for him. However, as a parent, I am encouraged by the words found in James 1:12: "Blessed is the man who perseveres under trial, because when he has stood the test, he will receive the crown of life that God has promised to those who love him" (NIV).

So who will be blessed? Those who persevere.

In this verse, although it was not specifically written with reference to parenting, James encourages us to not give in to temptation—not only temptations to sin but any temptations that go against what glorifies God. When I thought about temptations from a parenting perspective, several things came to mind: The temptation not to worry about what my kids watch on television because the world is saturated with bad language, sexual images, and violence everywhere anyway. The temptation to overlook dishonesty rather than taking time to discuss the importance of character and integrity and to implement discipline as needed. The temptation to allow my teenagers to go wherever they want to go just so I won't be the "mean mom" who always says no. The temptation to avoid deep conversations about drugs, alcohol, and sexual purity because they are not fun subjects to talk about.

The temptation to hold onto disappointment, hurt, or resentment when my children make mistakes, instead of forgiving and loving unconditionally. The temptation to lose my temper rather than practice self-control and patience. The temptation to let the church teach my children about God instead of making faith and prayer a priority in our home.

As we persevere through all the stress that comes along with raising children, we can have hope in knowing that God is always working behind the scenes in our children's lives, while we are planting seeds for fruit in their hearts along the way. But seed planting requires great perseverance.

I vividly remember one particularly stressful day about a year ago when both of my teenage daughters were in their rooms in an aftermath of charged emotions, while I was feeling overwhelmed with my own. So I did the only thing I could think of to do—I retreated to my front porch to be alone and to pray.

It had been yet another dramatic day in a household with maturing teenage girls. One was upset because she was not allowed to attend a social outing that "everybody else" was going to but that I just didn't have a good feeling about. The other was upset because of a recent breakup with a boyfriend and had become more emotional when I tried to console her.

Leading up to this stressful day, we had spent weeks dealing with a couple of very mean girl bullies at school who had made it a personal life goal to start hurtful rumors and cause heartache to innocent girls, one of whom was my daughter. My anger at these individuals, my heartache for my daughter, and my frustration with how the school system was handling the issue (or not handling it) had turned my nerves into a knotted mass. Not to mention the ongoing friend/ex-friend issues, fitting in, self-esteem, fashion woes, cheerleading drama, daily sports practices, and peer pressure situations that bobbed in and out of our lives every day like small ships tossed in stormy seas. And that's just the tip of the iceberg.

The stress of parenting had worn me down. I longed for some peace and quiet, and, although I would have loved to escape my problems by hopping on a plane to a Caribbean beach for the day, I knew what I really needed was to be alone with my feelings and with God. So, on the front porch I sat, soaking in the sunshine and secretly longing for the days gone by when things seemed so much easier and less stressful, to say the least.

As I breathed in the aroma of the spring air, watching the bumblebees drawing nectar from the flowers and listening to the birds sweetly chirping, my eyes fell upon a piece of the past. Tucked shallowly in the pine straw beside the front porch steps, under the shadow of a huge holly tree, were two faded, slightly cracked, plastic Easter eggs.

My thoughts were instantly jerked back to many years ago, when my daughters were small. My mind played out a memory, as if it were happening right in front of my eyes. I watched two dainty, blonde-headed, blue-eyed little beauties frolicking in the thick, green grass, wearing frilly white and pink Easter dresses, holding hands as they skipped. I could see their little fingers wrapped tightly around their wicker Easter baskets as they excitedly hid brightly colored Easter eggs around the yard and under the holly bushes—bushes that were then twelve inches tall but now stood at twelve feet.

To my own surprise, tears began trickling down my face. Things seemed so easy when my little girls thought I was the most wonderful person in the universe, and the hardest question of the day was whether they could have a snack before dinner. But, as I grappled with my emotions, I began to wonder if all the stress of parenting was even worth it. If trying to stand firm in my commitment to raise my children in the ways of the Lord—even if they didn't like it and even if other parents thought I was an over-protective Jesus freak—would ever pay off.

God is always faithful, and in this moment of self-doubt, he knew the reassurance I needed to hear. I sensed his whisper through the soft breeze that tousled my hair, reminding me that he had called me to be more than a mommy. He called me to be a mom who raises her children according to his Word, even when it's not easy. A mom who perseveres through the stress because of her commitment to raise children who know the Lord. A mom who sticks to her convictions, even when it would be easier and much less stressful to give in and just let them do what "everybody else" is doing. A mom who sleeps soundly at night, knowing she made good decisions for the well-being of her children, even if those children go to bed mad at her.

As I thought about all these things, reminiscing on the past and breathing in the present, my two precious teenage daughters discovered my hidden whereabouts on the porch. As we all three sat on the steps together, Kaitlyn ironically pointed out the eggs under the tree and my tears flowed again. Both of my girls looked at each other with perplexed expressions and then looked at me as if I had sprouted horns. *Why is Mom crying over an old, faded Easter egg?*

Then we all started laughing, shared some much-needed hugs, and spent the next half hour talking openly about feelings, life, and outfits for the next day. I suddenly felt a feeling of peace, knowing that God had given me a glimpse of the past so that I could embrace today and tomorrow with confidence as I persist in my quest to be the mom he called me to be. Although I know I am an imperfect mom raising imperfect kids, I believe God calls us to love our children enough to sometimes swim against the current.

Those faded Easter eggs were a symbol of what life once was but a sweet reminder that, even though the seasons of life may change, God never does. He is always there to help us stand strong and bring us peace when we need it most in our parenting journey, whether we are enduring sleepless nights and changing poopy diapers or enforcing curfews and molding hearts.

Parenting is stressful—in more ways than one—but through our perseverance and commitment to staying strong in our beliefs, despite whether everyone else is, we will be able to experience the joy discussed in 3 John 1:4, which says, "I have no greater joy than to hear that my children are walking in the truth" (NIV).

It's hard being a Christian in a lost and broken world, and it's even harder being a Christian parent. The truth is, even the best, most committed parenting efforts are not a guarantee that our children won't mess up. But when they do, as a result of standing firm in our faith, we will have practiced the art of persevering through difficult times and be better equipped to handle problems in a way that will be pleasing to God.

If you are suffering with parental exhaustion, you are not alone. But if you are wondering if you can survive another stressful day, maybe it's time you enjoy a little sabbatical on your front porch and ask God for perseverance to be the mom, or dad, God called you to be.

In the same way, the journey to becoming less stressed in a busy, chaotic, stress-driven culture is equally difficult as being a Christian parent. Trying to swim against the current norm of society and learn to depend on Jesus for peace instead of the ways of the world is even harder.

In either circumstance, Jesus holds the peace we long for. And, even if nobody else is looking for it and everybody else is going with the flow, we will always know where real peace can be found.

✍ Reflection Questions

1. What practical stress relief methods have you tried? How did these make you feel?

2. Have the worldly stress-relief tactics that you have tried provided any stress relief at all? If so, was that relief temporary and superficial, or permanent and life changing?

3. What unhealthy habits or possibly harmful methods of coping with your stress have you developed over time?

4. What healthy changes can you begin making today to better cope with your stress? Ask God for the wisdom and strength to overcome unhealthy habits and begin forming new habits that will result in positive change. Write out your prayerful thoughts here.

5. Do you believe that the key to managing your stress, and regaining your peace and joy, begins with Christ? Set aside some time to focus on God's promises about peace. Consider looking up these verses and ask God to speak to your heart through them: Psalm 16:8, Psalm 18:1–2, Psalm 18:6 , 2 Samuel 22:7, Matthew 11:28–30. 2 Corinthians 4:16–18, Ecclesiastes 7:14, and Psalm 46:1.

6. Are you possibly suffering from a case of parental exhaustion? If so, invite God into the picture, and ask him for peace in the midst of your stressful parenting "stuff."

7. Have you been tempted to take a back seat in your teenager's life, simply because it seems like it would be less stressful? If your answer is yes, consider making a list of the pros and cons of taking a back seat, and ask God to help you see why sometimes the toughest road is the one which leads to the greatest blessings.

If you have allowed the frustration and stress of parenting to keep you from being the parent you feel called to be, ask God to give you clarity about changes you can make to get back on track, the spiritual courage to stand firm in your Christian parenting beliefs even when it's hard, and the emotional strength to persevere.

Stress Busting Scriptures

The LORD is a refuge for the oppressed, a stronghold in times of trouble.
Those who know your name will trust in you, for you, LORD, have never
forsaken those who seek you.

Psalm 9:9–10 NIV

You are my hiding place; you will protect me from trouble and surround me
with songs of deliverance. I will instruct you and teach you in the way you
should go; I will counsel you and watch over you.

Psalm 32:7–8 NIV

This is what the Sovereign LORD, the Holy One of Israel, says:
"In repentance and rest is your salvation, in quietness and trust is your
strength, but you would have none of it."

Isaiah 30:15 NIV

"For I know the plans I have for you," says the LORD. "They are plans for
good and not for disaster, to give you a future and a hope."

Jeremiah 29:11

Rejoice in our confident hope. Be patient in trouble, and keep on praying.

Romans 12:12

Chapter Four

Time for Change

Just before quitting my job many years ago, I was already at the breaking point when the final blow was inflicted. The hit was hard—my boss informed me that I would soon be required to work more hours in the office—it pushed me over the edge towards serious life change. Since my employment there had already reached an unbearable stage, evidenced by daily bouts of nausea and tears shed, this news felt like a stake in my heart. I finally had to accept the reality that this place was not where God wanted me to be. So, after much discussion and prayer, my husband and I agreed that it would be in my best interest (and that of my family and my sanity) to take a leap of faith and resign.

As strange as it may sound, the idea of giving up my career and my income caused me even more anxiety than I was already dealing with, despite knowing that stress and misery had become the heartbeat of my daily existence. So, after weeks of inner turmoil, juggling my options and my fears like spinning plates balanced on sticks, I hesitantly and reluctantly decided to resign.

Even though I was very uncomfortable in this job, the thought of being unemployed was even more uncomfortable. I had been employed since graduating from college. I had always been a "working mom." My job was my identity (at least that's how I felt at the time). I thought my career defined who I was and gave me value in this world. I had not yet discovered that my true value and worth came from Christ alone, not from my name on a paycheck. And I certainly did not know that this drastic, sacrificial change that God had called me to make would help me discover the new me, a reflection of who he was. He had waited years for me to obey, and I finally surrendered.

You see, I had felt a call on my heart five years earlier to leave my job and focus on serving in ministry, but I had pushed that idea aside as ludicrous and absurd. God had been trying to get my attention, and finally, when I was at my lowest state (physically and emotionally), I was not only ready to listen but ready to obey. I figured nothing could be worse than the existence I was already enduring.

Ironically, against what the normal person would probably feel at the idea of taking a permanent vacation from work, the thought of quitting my job caused my stress levels to temporarily skyrocket. As I typed out my resignation letter, my stomach felt like I had swallowed ten pounds of granite, and the knot in my throat made it hard to swallow.

The devil filled my head with a million reasons why I should fight for my career: how I would feel lost and useless without a corporate job title to boost my importance in this world, why I should overlook my health issues, why I should not consider making my children and husband a priority, and why I should definitely have no interest in ministry.

As I succumbed to those lies from the enemy over a period of several weeks, my insecurities and fears became more and more overwhelming. I had given the devil a foothold in my heart, and he was kicking me down as hard as he could.

I fearfully pondered the thought of giving up everything I had worked so many years to achieve. I worried about losing the friends that I had made at work. I wondered if my parents would be disappointed in me, especially after forking out so much money on a college education.

I worried about how my husband and I could survive on one income. I worried about the reality of actually having no income and being totally financially dependent on my husband, causing me to break out in a cold sweat at the sheer thought of being a submissive wife. I even secretly wondered if there was a "shoppers anonymous" support group near my home, convinced that I would need it.

But I loved my children immensely and wanted to be home with them. I was excited about the opportunity to actually get to see them more than a couple hours a day. I had always admired and secretly envied moms who had chosen to stay home and raise their children. I loved my husband and wanted to be a loving wife—not a stressed-out, agitated, worn-out wife all the time.

I also loved my Jesus and now knew without a shadow of a doubt that he had called me to follow him down a new path, even though I was scared to death to actually take it and had no idea where that path would lead.

But, despite what my heart was telling me, I simply could not envision myself as a stay-at-home mom, a person serving in ministry, or a fully devoted housewife. I was too stressed to allow myself to consider what God might have in store for me, so my mind became engulfed with fears and what-ifs.

Yet, with quivering fingers and mixed emotions, I pushed past my fear and doubts and finally turned in my resignation. With each passing day of my six-week resignation period, God gently drew me closer and closer, reassuring me that his plans were better than mine, even though I could not understand them yet. He poured people into my path to encourage me in my choices—people that I had worked with for years and never even knew were believers.

God knew that a positive change in my life was long overdue, and I finally came to a place in my heart and mind where I agreed. I was finally *ready* to be set free from the prison of stress that I had been living in and embrace what his plans were once and for all.

When Change Seems Strange

The first couple months of being voluntarily unemployed were, shall I say, very strange. I felt as if I didn't know who I was. I hardly knew what to do with myself. I would wake up in the morning and scurry around to get the children ready for school, but once they were gone I was like a little puppy lost in a field of hundreds of acres.

I felt disconnected from what used to be my life, from people, from business meetings, from goals, and from adult interaction. I could not get my head out of the game. I spoke with someone from my old office every day just to see what was going on, who was doing what, how the search was going for my replacement, and what office politics were still running rampant. I was sure that I still needed to be plugged in to find any self-worth at all.

But then the strangeness of change began to feel less strange, and I began to experience some refreshing changes. A few months after resigning, I began to see the little glimmer of light that God had been waving in front of my eyes all along like the beam from a lighthouse far off in the distance. As I adjusted to my new lifestyle at home, away from my leather chair, high-rise office, oh-so-important responsibilities, and overwhelming office issues, my stress slowly began to dissipate.

I gradually grew to love being at home, basking in my newfound freedom to be who I wanted to be, and not who a corporation expected me to be. I enjoyed not having to constantly defend and justify my abilities and my character. I also realized the damage that had been done to my self-esteem as a result of working for someone who treated me as an inferior human being. Needless to say, I loved the fact that I could now look to my new Boss for confirmation of my worth—Jesus himself. And this Boss adored me so much that he had given his life for me.

After that period of adjustment, I began to realize that I had been on a corporate train wreck for years and never even tried to escape, similar to being on that spinning merry-go-round. I had not recognized the emotional prison that I had been willingly trapped in. Stress and chaos used to be my normal, but now God was blessing me with the new normal that he knew was best all along.

My excitement grew about embracing the life that God had in store for me. As my faith blossomed and I devoted more time to my relationship with Christ, he lovingly proceeded to give me tiny glimpses of the wonderful plans he had for me, just as he promised in Jeremiah 29:11 when he said, "For I know the plans I have for you. . . . They are plans for good and not for disaster, to give you a future and a hope."

I began taking little steps of faith to do what I knew God had called me to do years earlier. I devoted many hours trying to learn how to be a Christian speaker and writer and how to get that goal off the ground. Now that I was seeking God's guidance, instead of following my own agenda for worldly success, I was able to dedicate my time and energies to the things that really mattered.

Over time, I slowly began to see some other strange changes. Not just in my stress level, my faith walk and my overall emotional health, but in my physical health as well. At first it seemed peculiar, and it took me a few months to figure out what was going on. Then one day, out of the blue, I noticed something absolutely amazing—I had risen from my bed after a good night's sleep and felt a strange sensation, a new zest and energy for the day. I was ready to get up and get moving and felt enthusiastic about the things I planned to do that day. Then it hit me. I simply felt . . . good. In fact, I felt great! What in the world was this strange phenomenon of feeling good, healthy, and happy?!

I suddenly realized that I was no longer facing endless daily health challenges. It dawned on me that it had been weeks since I even thought about whether I was going to live to a ripe old age. Then, as if a light bulb switched on in my mind, I became acutely aware that I was miraculously less stressed . . . and it felt incredible! It had been so long since I had been less stressed, I had forgotten how it felt to be happy and at peace. And trust me, friends, it was a good, good feeling that came solely because of the powerful presence of God in my life and the fact that I was now walking in obedience to his will, instead of my own.

If you glean only one point of wisdom from this entire book, let it be this: less stress does not come from removing yourself from a stressful job. You truly become less stressed when you discover the God of peace.

The real peace comes when you make God the center of your life, instead of the last resort, and when you begin focusing on what God has called you to do, instead of what you have set out to do within the restrictions of your own agenda or skill set. My stress lessened when I turned to God for stress relief, instead of to the ways of society. Most importantly, stress relief became a reality when two little words crossed my lips . . . *Yes, Lord.* God had waited years to hear me utter those words, and I can't help but assume that my life would have been much less stressed all along if only I had listened and surrendered to his ways sooner.

Called to Change

Several years before all this stress erupted at work like a volcano with a vengeance, God had placed a call upon my life, which I had blatantly and consciously ignored. Let's backtrack for a moment and delve into the details of where my journey first began.

It all started one beautiful spring day when I found myself at a women's ministry seminar at my church. Although I was attending church regularly at the time, I was more of a pew dweller than an active Christian. I had never participated in a women's church function before. But for reasons I didn't know at the time (which in hindsight could only have been the nudging of the Holy Spirit) I felt a desire to go to this seminar. I had every intention of enjoying a Saturday morning to myself, free from crying little ones and dirty laundry. I planned on singing some praise and worship songs, listening to a typical message of encouragement, eating refreshments, and sharing a few laughs with friends. I certainly did not expect anything out of the ordinary to occur, but God had something extraordinary planned.

As I sat there in the sanctuary, listening to the speaker share her powerful, life-changing testimony, I felt the presence of God stronger than ever before. At the time, it was a new feeling for me, and I couldn't quite understand what I was experiencing. I had heard people talk about feeling the presence of the Holy Spirit but had never experienced it for myself so had decided that type of thing only happened to holy rollers—which I certainly was not.

Despite my skepticism, I knew what I was feeling had to be God. It was heavy, yet light. Suffocating, yet freeing. Nerve-racking, yet peaceful. I felt as if I could reach out and touch him right then and there. You see, when I walked into that sanctuary wearing a big smile on my face, I was hiding a heart that was shattered. I had spent years feeling worthless—like a broken, throwaway person because of the sins in my past. I felt void of any value. Unredeemable. Unlovable. Unforgivable. Despicable in God's eyes.

Upon hearing the speaker's testimony, which was astonishingly similar to my own—the deep, raw wounds in my heart became exposed. The windows of my soul were flung wide open, and God could reach down to even the darkest parts. I was sobbing and praying for God to forgive me for past sins—sins that had held me captive in guilt and shame for years, sins that had kept my stress level at an all-time high as I harbored them in my heart and ensnared them with my own insecurities, sins that had caused me to believe the lies of the enemy. The enemy who had convinced me day after day that God could never forgive someone like me, much less love me or have a purpose for me. As I begged for God's forgiveness once again, I felt his mercy and compassion flooding over me like surging waters.

In this sweet, powerful moment with God, while my requests for his love and forgiveness still hung in the air, I felt his power wash through my soul and the weight of my sin being lifted away. I could feel the difference in my heart, and my spiritual ears were awakened for the very first time.

Instantly, I was overcome with praise, gratitude, and awe. I wanted to stand up and shout out to the heavens with open arms, publicly expressing my thankfulness and reverence. But for fear of what others might think of me, I stayed motionless and paralyzed in my pew.

As I relished in the freedom that I had just received, my heart ached to hear a divine message reassuring me that the feelings I was experiencing were real. As I sat there in the pew, eyes closed, spiritual ears open, hot tears stinging my face and bursting forth like water from a dam that had just given way to the pressure—it happened.

Suddenly, the Lord's voice echoed so loudly that it startled me. My eyes thrust open and I glanced around to see if anyone else had heard it. Since I saw no commotion in the sanctuary, and no other women appearing to be confused, alarmed, or frantically gazing upwards with a look of *Who said that!?* on their faces, I determined that I was, indeed, the only one who had heard his voice. It was a divine message, meant for me alone.

I was actually stunned to think God had spoken to little ol' me. I thought that only happened in books or movies, not in real life. I thought that only happened to people who were thoroughly spiritual and righteous—not to pathetic sinners like me. The sheer thought that God had paused in his job of running the universe to lean down and speak peace, truth, and purpose into a broken-hearted, stressed-out young woman's heart stopped me in my tracks.

He had spoken, and I had heard. He was loud, yet he was silent. Gently but firmly, God spoke four little words that would forever alter the course of my life. He simply said, *"Tracie, go . . . and share."* As I sat there stunned, my mind raced with thoughts not only because I had heard God's audible voice in my spirit but because I was confused . . . *go where?* and *share what?*

His answer to my questions were much more subtle but just as clear. The realization of what he was calling me to do left me speechless. You see, he was calling me to go to a new place and to trust him to lead the way. He was calling me to quit my job—a job which was causing me too much stress anyway but which I had never contemplated leaving. He was calling me to share the painful memories of my past with other women who needed to hear a message of hope and forgiveness. He was calling me to help other women discover the transforming peace that I had just received.

But instead of allowing my thankfulness for who he was to fuel me with courage and passion, I was overcome with a sudden sensation of debilitating fear when I considered what "going" and "sharing" really meant. So, as my fears overshadowed my gratitude, I quickly and adamantly answered God's call by saying, *"No."* There was absolutely no way I could ever have the courage to do that—not even twenty seconds' worth.

As honored and humbled as I was to have experienced such a divine God encounter, I had never intended for my life to be interrupted that day. I simply had no interest in carrying out the plan for my life that God had just laid out in my heart. I had a career to consider and a salary that I depended on. So what if I was stressed? Did it really matter? Just the thought of following his call made me feel weak in the knees. The idea of being transparent and vulnerable—open to judgment and criticism, becoming the brunt of jokes, being the subject of whispers of gossip, talking in front of groups of people—made me feel physically ill.

Although I walked out of the sanctuary that morning a transformed woman on the inside, I was too terrified to obey his call on the outside. I turned my back on his plan and began walking down the winding road of life that I thought seemed like the better choice. A life that would be so consumed with twists and turns and overwhelming stress that it would leave my head spinning.

I chose a life of stress instead of the sweet life God had designed for me for two reasons. The first reason was that I had failed to ever build a strong relationship with Christ. Although I had spoken the words to accept Jesus Christ as my Savior as a child, I was more of a churchgoer than a true Christ "follower." I had spent years going through the motions of Christianity, oblivious to the fact that I had a religion, not a relationship.

The second reason was that I was just too afraid to trust God with my life—a sure sign of a lack of relationship with Christ. I was unsure if he was really capable of providing and protecting or if he really had a plan for a broken woman like me. My feelings of unworthiness compounded my fears, and, as a result, I did not know how to trust God, and I certainly didn't know he was the answer to my stress.

If only I had known how beautiful God's path would be or possessed the faith to honestly believe that his plan was better than mine. But, as a result of the lack of an intimate relationship with Christ, I spent the next five years running as far in the other direction as I could from his plan.

I ran back into my high-rise building, back to following a career dream that God never intended for me in the first place, and back to thinking that happiness would come with a big salary and a big corporate agenda.

All of the adversity and stress that I encountered during those five years of disobedience are what you read about in the previous chapters. All those years that I spent drowning in stress and health problems could have been prevented if only I had said, *"Yes, Lord"* much sooner. His peace had been available to me throughout my whole ordeal, but it took me letting go of the rope and plunging into the pit before I decided that maybe, just maybe, his ways were better.

As I look back on my life now, it is so obvious that my stress really didn't come from the external pressures of my job, the hurtful people in my life, or the difficult adversities that I faced. My stress resulted from not knowing God, not trusting him with my whole heart, seeking peace and purpose from the world instead of from him, and from being so afraid of change that I would rather suffer than obey.

Afraid of Change

When I left that moving worship service on that life-changing day, I knew I could never deny that God had spoken. But I was still afraid. Afraid of the past. Afraid of the future. Afraid to write and to speak publicly, especially about matters of faith (matters on which I was no expert). Afraid of being transparent and being hurt, and of feeling ashamed. Afraid of ridicule and of sacrifice.

Afraid of what God might call me to do next and of what God might do as a result of my disobedience. Afraid to walk down the path that God had been preparing for me my whole life. Afraid to take a chance on God and to get to know him too closely, because an intimate relationship might force me out of my comfort zone. Afraid to obey.

Afraid to change.

But being the loving, gentle, and patient heavenly Father that he is, God waited. And when I was finally ready to surrender my life of stress for his life of blessing, he took me by the hand and led the way. He held me up during my transition from working mom to just mom. He escorted me away from feeling like I needed to be someone important in the eyes of the corporate world to knowing that I was important in the eyes of Christ—the only One whose approval I ever really needed.

He helped me embrace the reality that my true value was in him, not in what I was doing each day at an office. He helped me learn to trust that he would provide for my family, even when finances didn't seem to be enough and logical number crunching just didn't add up. He opened the eyes of my heart so I could clearly see him at work, gleaning spiritual insight into what his will was for my life. The Prince of Peace poured peace into all the empty spaces in my heart that had once been filled with stress.

I escaped the prison of stress that I had been living in not only because I found the God of peace but because I also discovered that he was my best friend and that all he ever wanted for me was his normal.

If God's plan for me had included remaining in the corporate world, then I would still be there, serving him in the mission field of corporate America. I have a wonderful friend who loves her job and witnesses to more people in her office in a week than most people to do on an overseas mission trip. She knows that she is exactly where God called her to be, and she is living out God's call each and every day. On Sundays, she serves as one of my small-group Bible study leaders, and her passion for Christ exudes from her heart with every lesson she teaches.

God does not call each of his children to leave their careers behind as he did me, but he definitely has a uniquely designed plan for each one. He calls each of us to serve him in the unique way, and in the unique places, that he has equipped us to glorify him in.

Many of you reading this book have wonderful careers and feel confident that it is exactly where God has called you to be. I pray God is blessing your hard work and commitment and that you feel his affirmation in what you are doing while shining his light through you on the people that he has put in your path. Regardless of whether you work in a corporate high-rise or a home office, as stay-at-home mom or dad, in a warehouse, at the mall, in ministry, on the mission field, or on staff at a church—if you are in God's unique and destined will for your life and are making your relationship with him a priority, you can keep stress at bay because real peace will take up residence in your heart.

Reflection Questions

1. What changes could you make in your life that might eliminate stress? List them here.

2. Regarding the changes you listed above, what obstacles might stand in the way? How can you proactively prepare to overcome those obstacles?

3. Are your secret fears, insecurities, or past sins preventing you from making necessary changes that would help alleviate some of your stressors? What can you do to start trusting God with your whole heart and your whole life and start accepting how valuable you are to him?

4. What steps can you take today to begin tackling your fears and moving forward in faith? Consider these verses when answering that question: 1 Chronicles 28:20, Psalm 27:1, Psalm 56:3–4, Isaiah 41:13, Isaiah 54:4, 2 Timothy 1:7, Hebrews 13:5–6.

5. Have you ever wondered if there is more to life than what you are currently doing? Is it possible you have been too stressed and distracted to consider that God might have a better plan for you? If so, take a moment to jot down any God-sized dreams that have been hidden in your heart, no matter how impossible or farfetched they may seem. Pray for God to make it clear what your next steps should be, remembering that God only asks that we take one step at a time, trusting him along the way.

> *Faith is taking the first step even when*
> *you don't see the whole staircase.*
> Martin Luther King Jr.

6. Have you ever knowingly told God "no"? Write about something you need to say, "Yes, Lord" to.

7. Has God ever prompted you to make a change in your life, and when you obeyed, you could see that his ways were best? Write down those spiritual markers in your life and spend time thanking God for using all things to his glory. Let them serve as encouragement for trusting God with your future.

Stress Busting Scriptures

Don't copy the behavior and customs of this world, but let God transform you into a new person by changing the way you think. Then you will learn to know God's will for you, which is good and pleasing and perfect.

Romans 12:2

Then [Jesus] said, "I tell you the truth, unless you turn from your sins and become like little children, you will never get into the Kingdom of Heaven."

Matthew 18:3

That is why the LORD says, "Turn to me now, while there is time. Give me your hearts. Come with fasting, weeping, and mourning. Don't tear your clothing in your grief, but tear you hearts instead." Return to the LORD your God, for he is merciful and compassionate, slow to get angry and filled with unfailing love. He is eager to relent and not punish.

Joel 2:12–13

It is better to take refuge in the LORD than to trust in people.

Psalm 118:8

*O LORD, I give my life to you. I trust in you, my God!
Do not let me be disgraced, or let my enemies rejoice in my defeat.*

Psalm 25:1–2

Chapter Five

Take Back Your Life

Have you ever wondered who you really are, or where the person went that you used to be? Have you ever dreamed about the person you wanted to be but felt unable to become that person because of circumstances in your life, pressures on your heart, sins of your past, or the weight of daily chaos? Do you wish you could relax in a beach chair and spend a few hours submerging your feet in the gentle waves lapping on the shore, but you are stretched too thin to even consider a moment's rest?

Maybe you have vague recollections of a time when you were footloose and fancy-free, lying in soft grass on a beautiful spring day and watching the clouds go by as you tried to figure out which ones looked like recognizable shapes. Or maybe you love to reminisce about distant childhood memories of swinging on a rope swing in your grandmother's backyard, picking up pecans from the pecan trees, and frolicking around in the sprinkler in the hot sun. A smile may come to your face as you think back to the awesome sense of freedom surging through your spirit as you rode your bicycle through your neighborhood or played hide-and-seek with your friends until you heard your mom calling you home for dinner.

Ahhhh, those were the days. If you had a relatively normal childhood, you may remember those simple, carefree days too. The days when we were young, with no jobs or financial worries, and our only concerns were whether we were going to be invited to the popular kid's birthday party.

I like to imagine what it would be like to go back to those laid-back and worry-free days. Sometimes, as I watch my teenage daughters scurrying through life, I feel a little envious. They are so full of energy and filled with excitement about what each new day brings no matter how small or insignificant. They spend their time counting down the weeks until summer vacation, hanging out with their friends, and making plans for college careers. Funny how when we are young, we never envision ourselves living a life bogged down with chaos and stress, void of adventure and excitement. But unfortunately, as we grow up, our stress grows at an even faster rate, threatening to steal our joy and peace, especially if we lose sight of our sense of innocent enthusiasm and our childlike faith.

On the other hand, maybe your childhood isn't something you want to reminisce about at all. Maybe you struggle to remember any times of peace in days gone by. Maybe you suffered from physical or sexual abuse as a child, mental and emotional abuse, or neglect and a lack of feeling loved or accepted. Maybe you had an abortion as a young woman and have never been able to shake the shame or remorse. Maybe your family struggled financially, or divorce wreaked havoc on your home.

Maybe you feel as if the pain in your heart that has evolved over a lifetime of hard experiences prevents you from even being able to fathom having a life of peace, much less a heart full of joy. Maybe you would never in a million years want to relive your childhood, because it was more stressful than your life today. Could those memories of difficult times possibly be adding to your current stress, even if you think you have dealt with those emotions?

Whether our childhood was peaceful, chaotic, or painful, it doesn't have to dictate how we live our lives today. We can believe that a life of peace and less stress is feasible if we rely on our God, who promises that it can be.

Mark 10:27 says, "Jesus looked at them intently and said, 'Humanly speaking, it is impossible. But not with God. Everything is possible with God.'" Living a life full of joy and void of pain may seem impossible to you today, humanly speaking, as you find yourself pondering all the difficult situations in your life—the hardships you have endured, the pain you have experienced, the struggles you are currently facing, or the looming hopelessness of the future. But true joy and peace are within your reach if you are reaching out to the right place for help—Jesus Christ. Peace is not a matter of life or circumstances; it's a matter of the heart.

God could change our circumstances at any time, if he chose to do so, but he is always more interested in changing us *through* our circumstances than changing our circumstances themselves. Everything is possible with God, because he said so.

When God Seems Absent

There are countless stories in the Bible of people who faced great adversity and stress but who persevered in Christ, finding peace and blessing as a result. One of those people can be found in the book of 1 Samuel, and her name was Hannah.

When we are introduced to Hannah, we find out that she was one of Elkanah's two wives; the other wife was Peninnah. Even though having more than one wife was a common practice in biblical times, Hannah's stress probably began at the onset of having to share her husband with another woman. I simply cannot imagine how emotionally challenging that must have been.

Though an accepted practice in biblical times, polygamy was never God's intention for marriage when he instituted it in the Garden of Eden. Women were not meant to have to share husbands, and God did not create them to be robots with no emotions. Marriage was created to be a loving, monogamous union between one man and one woman, where adultery was forbidden and divorce was not an option.

This society that condoned polygamy was part of the culture that Hannah lived in and obviously caused her tumultuous stress and heartache. However, the real stressor for Hannah is revealed in 1 Samuel 1:2 when we read that while her co-wife, Peninnah, had children, Hannah's struggle with infertility left her childless. According to 1 Samuel 1:3, it is implied that her infertility had been going on for years, leaving Hannah in daily anguish. It also says that each year, Elkanah, along with Hannah and Peninnah with all her kids in tow, would travel to Shiloh to worship and offer sacrifices. This is where Hannah's heartache would be manifested in its highest form.

You see, each year when they would travel to Shiloh, and probably on a day-in and day-out basis, Peninnah would torment Hannah with words of ridicule. 1 Samuel 1:6–7 says, "So Peninnah would taunt Hannah and make fun of her because the LORD had kept her from having children. Year after year it was the same—Peninnah would taunt Hannah as they went to the Tabernacle. Each time, Hannah would be reduced to tears and would not even eat."

Hannah was tormented not only because of the stigma and shame of being barren and the emptiness in her heart caused by her lack of children but also because of the great persecution that was mercilessly bestowed upon her by Peninnah. After years of anguish, the day finally came when Hannah had all she could take. Even when Elkanah saw her crying and refusing to eat and reminded her how happy she should be because he was devoted to her and her needs (verse 8), she absolutely could not contain her overwhelming sorrow anymore.

She had had quite enough of Peninnah and her self-centered, inconsiderate, hurtful ways. She was tired of the emotional abuse and endless ridicule that Peninnah inflicted upon her. She was fed up with always being treated as an inferior woman because of circumstances beyond her control. She was tired of feeling ashamed, broken, empty-hearted, and empty-handed.

Her emotions must have surely ravaged her heart to the core. I can only assume that she tried to be happy that Elkanah loved her, especially knowing how much he obviously adored her. I bet she tried to stay focused on her blessings rather than being consumed with yearning for the blessings she had yet to receive. I can also imagine how helpless she must have felt to remedy this problem. All of these things combined most likely ushered her into a deep pit of hopelessness, where peace escaped her. And I feel certain that, when she was at her lowest point, Peninnah was there to continue with her emotional lashings.

We read in verses 6 and 7 that Hannah had been going to the place of worship year after year, as was the custom, but this year, *something* was different. Hannah was stressed beyond belief. She was at the end of her rope. She desperately needed something to change.

She had been faithful and trusting of her Lord and had prayed for a child for years to no avail. She was in a place of complete dependence on God, because he was the only hope she had left. She wanted less of her and more of God; and in her inconsolable despondency, she called out to him.

She said, as noted in 1 Samuel 1:11, "O LORD Almighty, if you will only look upon your servant's misery and remember me" (NIV). Hannah was desperate to know that God saw her and her pain. She needed to be noticed. She wanted to be remembered. She wanted to be touched by God, and she wanted resolution to her stress.

Although Hannah had prayed about this problem before, probably hundreds of times, God had still not answered her prayers for a child. However, on this particular day, she was so desperate for God's intervention that she dropped to her knees and poured out her entire heart. She held nothing back and laid all of her feelings and emotions at his feet. She was ready to take back her life, lay down her stress, and accept whatever plan God had for her.

She was so absolutely destitute and broken that she not only prayed but she prayed with fervency, gusto, and enthusiasm. She prayed out of her distress and great need with such passion and intensity that onlookers thought she was drunk. When Eli, the high priest, questioned her behavior, she answered in verses 15 and 16 by saying, "Oh no, sir! . . . I haven't been drinking wine or anything stronger. But I am very discouraged, and I was pouring out my heart to the LORD. Don't think I am a wicked woman! For I have been praying out of great anguish and sorrow." God then spoke through Eli, and he said to Hannah in verse 17, "Go in peace! May the God of Israel grant the request you have asked of him."

Hannah did have great faith, even though she felt weak at the time having endured so many years of adversity and torment from her co-wife. But, when Hannah received a word of encouragement from Eli, she believed she had been given a message from God. Eli was a well-respected priest and judge, loved and admired by all who knew him. So when he spoke, people listened. She hung on his every word. In verse 18, Hannah responded to Eli by saying, "Oh, thank you, sir!" Then we are told she went back and began to eat and was no longer sad.

Why was she no longer sad? Why did she immediately regain her appetite? After all, she did not suddenly have a swollen pregnant belly. Her circumstances were exactly the same. She was still a co-wife of Elkanah, and she would still be traveling back home with that horrible Peninnah and all her kids.

So what was different? What had changed? The answer is Hannah's heart. Hannah had poured out her deepest hurts and longings to God and sincerely believed that he had heard them. She had no idea if, when, or how God would answer her prayers; but she believed that whatever happened would be good—his good and pleasing will, despite what that may be.

Hannah's faith was the answer to her stress. And, through that faith, she found peace, even though her life remained far from peaceful. Her faith resulted in God working on her behalf. Hannah did not find peace because she left a stressful situation—she found peace because she had learned to depend on God's strength to rise above her stress.

This story has a happy ending in 1 Samuel 1:19–20 where we read, "The entire family got up early the next morning and went to worship the LORD once more. Then they returned home to Ramah. When Elkanah slept with Hannah, the LORD remembered her plea, and in due time she gave birth to a son. She named him Samuel, for she said, 'I asked the LORD for him.'"

I love that God gave Hannah a happy ending, and I believe that our heavenly Father wants us all to have happy endings. It may not always be the ending that we asked for, but when we trust that God's ways are always best, we can feel confident in knowing that he's got us covered.

A key point found in verse 19, crucial to our own faith walk and our quest for peace, is when we read that "the LORD remembered her." He remembered the faithful woman who had continued to love him and worship him despite her years of painful circumstances and heartache. He remembered the faithful woman who had sought his help and continued to persevere even when it appeared God wasn't answering her prayers. He remembered the woman who knew that her only hope for a solution to her stress would be found in the One who had created her.

He remembered her, and, despite all the emotional and physical suffering that she endured, she had remembered him. It was Hannah's strong faith that opened the door for the Lord to work in her life, and her faith led to peace and blessings.

The Lord could have given her a child at any time, even upon her first request spoken years earlier right after marrying Elkanah. Instead, he spent years grooming her heart, building her dependence and desperation for him, and preparing her for his plans. In this case, his plans were for her to give birth to a son whom she would fully dedicate to the Lord.

Because of her faith, Hannah became a different person, even when her circumstances stayed the same. God could have intervened in Hannah's circumstances at any time, but he chose to change Hannah's heart instead—the same way he often does in our lives, as well.

No matter what adversities we face or how difficult our circumstances are, God remembers us. Take comfort in knowing that God has not left you, even if it seems like he is absent in your life or that he does not see or care about what you are going through.

As we make our faith a priority and learn to trust in God's plans even if we do not understand them or like them, the doors will be flung wide open for God to enter our lives and begin his mighty work. During the wait we are called to fall on our knees just like Hannah and pour out our hearts to him. We are each called to live life in a state of dependency on him, believing that his peace is available in any situation.

I have always heard that God is never late, he is seldom early, but he is always right on time. His timing is not our own. Hannah wanted a child for years, but God chose the perfect time, at his appointed moment, to bless her with one, in the scheme of his bigger picture. We may want many things that seem to be out of our reach, but trusting in God's timing gives us hope and strength to seek his peace during the wait.

But what should we do while we are waiting on God's perfect timing? What is our course of action after we place our circumstances into God's hands? The answer is not to sit idly by waiting on God to do something but to actively strive for a change of heart, just like Hannah. We must choose to expectantly wait for God to work in our lives. Rather than spend time pouting because he hasn't shown up or assume he does not care about us, we need to focus on believing that, in one way or another, his answer will come in his time.

True faith is not passive but active, and genuinely active faith requires focusing on the health of our entire being—spiritually and physically. As we discussed in Chapter Two, 1 Corinthians 3:16 reminds us that we are God's temples, and stress can tear down that temple from the inside out. By nurturing our faith and staying in tune with our bodies, we will be ready spiritually and physically to move with him when the time is right and according to his will. If any part of the temple is broken, true worship can never take place.

Your Body Can Talk

Turning our problems over to God and trusting that he remembers us, sees our issues, and desires to intervene in our lives in his perfect timing are pivotal in our quest to find less stress and more peace. But, in the meantime, we cannot afford to ignore physical warnings of destruction.

Our bodies give us loads of blinking signs to let us know when our stress is pushing us into the danger zone. Nobody knows your body as well as you do, so, once you learn to identify your own signs of stress, they can serve as your personal emergency broadcast system.

Hypothetically, consider that your body is an expensive, high-end car with a shiny exterior and all the finest bells and whistles. Since you have a lot invested in this car and want to keep it running properly, you know you have to keep a keen eye on the dashboard gauges, as they are your only way to know what's going on under the hood. You know that, even when things look perfectly normal and flawless on the outside, problems could be brewing without your knowledge, which you won't know about until an alarm sounds.

Our body has gauges too, as well as alarms, although our alarms do not exhibit themselves with sounds or blinking lights. While we would never ignore an obvious problem with our vehicle that could possibly cause us to be stranded on the side of the road, we are quick to ignore alarms that our body is sending—writing them off as more of a nuisance than an actual problem demanding our attention. However, ignoring these issues can cause us to become stranded along the highway of life and to possibly face a major, costly repair job. But if we are paying attention to what our bodies are telling us, we can quickly tend to a problem when it arises in the hopes of warding off future problems.

So what are the warning signs you should be looking for? How can you avoid having to go in for a major overhaul? How do you know if stress is taking a physical toll on you? Those warning signs vary from person to person. I have shared with you many of the symptoms that I experienced, but it certainly was not an all-inclusive list, because everyone's body reacts differently to stress.

Some symptoms of chronic stress issues could include things like changes in body functions; deterioration of your physical health; changes in moods, feelings, and emotions; crying at unusual times or over minor things; behavioral changes; increasing health issues; fatigue; inability to take deep breaths; irritability or increased anger; changes in eating habits; inability to sleep soundly; increased use of drugs or alcohol; abuse of prescription drugs; withdrawal from friends or family members; an inability to concentrate; and feeling hopeless or helpless.

A few more bothersome problems include headaches, stomach problems, muscle tension, teeth grinding, changes in sex drive, dizziness, feeling nervous or anxious all the time, severing relationships, and having a lack of energy.[15]

Unfortunately, there are a few statistics that are more heartbreaking than others. For example, 8 percent of people studied in a 2008 survey admitted that their stress had led to divorce or separation from their spouse.[16] It is also disturbing to read that more than fifty million prescriptions were filled in 2008 for sleeping pills.[17] Companies spend $300 billion each year on stress-related health-care issues and stress reduction in the workplace.[18] It is probably safe to assume that, considering the stressful state of our nation and world right now, these numbers have increased over the past few years.

Are you beginning to agree that stress is one of worst epidemics that has ever hit this country and the only life-threatening disease that is outright and purposely ignored? Isn't it amazing that an epidemic of these proportions is accepted as the norm and overlooked by everyone, including the people who are suffering the most? It's sad but true, yet the disease of stress cannot be ignored because in the worst-case scenario, doing so could have fatal consequences.

When we are operating in a constant high-stress mode, we may experience one bothersome symptom or an entire slew of them, but none of them should be ignored. I know myself well enough now to be able to recognize when stress is rearing its ugly head again; and I trust that soon you will also get to know your body and be on alert for your own warning signs before it's too late.

Fortunately, there is a vaccine for this disease of stress that can not only treat the majority of the symptoms but also potentially prevent them from occurring. It is a vaccine of hope found right smack in the middle of the words of Jesus Christ. When we inject these life-saving truths into our hearts, allowing them to course through our veins with healing strength, we will begin to see the life-changing power that the Bible really holds.

Troubles and Treasures

It was one of those times when I thought the worst was yet to come. I truly believed that Satan had dealt the final blow to my marriage. We had been married for many years, and, just like any marriage, we had gone through our fair share of hard times. The stress from everyday life, relationships, finances, parenting, lack of time, disagreements, differences of opinions, distrust, hurt feelings, and so on, had taken its toll.

It seemed that no matter how much I sought after the Lord and prayed for my husband and my marriage, the problems persisted and our relationship remained strained. Despite my desire to respect and honor my husband as I knew God calls wives to do, the devil would constantly fill my head with an abundance of reasons why I had no real reason to do that.

You see, Satan had been hard at work for years trying to build walls between my husband and me. In every marriage, as soon as a couple says, "I do," the devil sets his sights on using his devious ways to tear the relationship apart. Marriage was the first union established by God, and if the devil can tear that apart, he might just take us down with it. Since children are negatively affected by divorce, he knows he can possibly turn their hearts against God, too. Satan does not like marriage, and he has been attacking the sanctity of marriage in our country with all the tools of his trade.

Unfortunately, for the first ten years of our married life, my husband and I did not make God the center of our marriage. I know now that when we leave any sort of opening for the devil to enter, in our hearts or in our marriages, he will march in full force ahead. It seemed that every time I turned around, there was yet another problem to deal with. The enemy had filled my head with lies, permeating my heart with insecurities and saturating my mind with resentment, and I had been listening intently. My thoughts would often spin with self-condemnation for my own flaws and failures as a wife, while also obsessing over all the flaws and failures of my husband. The enemy hoped that if we both felt worthless and beyond repair and angry and bitter towards each other, our marriage would surely crumble.

Over a process of several years, Satan continued to throw stumbling blocks into our paths, causing us to falter and fumble in our relationship. Despite the endless hours of prayer for my marriage, it felt as if my prayers were going nowhere. I was in a season of faith where I could relate to Hannah, wondering if God even remembered I was still down here on earth and if he cared about my pain at all. I had been praying for an improved marriage year after year, and honestly I was growing weary of the wait.

One particular day, after another round of arguments and facing a new and upsetting issue, I found myself in the deepest pit of despair that I could remember ever being in. I felt hurt and betrayed and my trust was shaken. Although I was actively pursuing my faith, I was beginning to lean towards passivity as my hope began to wane, and, upon letting down my guard, the devil jumped in. He began to fill my mind and my heart with a raging flurry of anger and fears. I had no idea how to handle, much less fix, the issues that now threatened our relationship.

One rainy Sunday afternoon, shortly after this new and troubling issue had presented itself in our lives, I found myself feeling especially sad, worried, and discouraged. It seemed like all the problems in the world were crashing down upon me all at once. I felt a weight so heavy on my heart, it was as if I could barely stand. But, as a mother of three young children who were always swarming around me, I had no choice but to bury my emotions and keep up the all-too-familiar charade that everything was fine.

I knew that, for the sake of my family, it would be inappropriate to have a meltdown, wallow in a puddle of tears, or bang my fists on the floor. Letting my emotions explode would have resulted in a whole new set of issues to deal with. Having grown up in a broken home and understanding the heartache that marital problems inflict on the whole family, I had always tried to avoid creating any of those types of worries in the minds of my own children. And this day was no different.

Since the rain had trapped us all inside and everyone was occupied with toys and television, I wandered quietly into the solace of my bedroom and gingerly closed the door. The room was unusually dim and gloomy for the time of day that it was, so I clicked on the lamp beside my bed. As the warm glow bathed the room in soft light, my eyes landed upon the gift that a precious Christian friend had given me just a few weeks earlier.

It was a small crystal box engraved with delicate designs, including a little heart right on the top, still snuggled in the puffy, yellow chiffon bow that had been lovingly placed around it. Some people have called it a "treasure box," others a "blessings box," but, no matter what you call it, it had become a heartfelt keepsake. Although it was a beautiful addition to my bedside table, it wasn't the physical beauty of the box that mattered at all but the beauty of the contents inside that I truly treasured.

This little glass box was filled with dozens of small, carefully folded slips of paper, and on each slip of paper was written an encouraging Bible verse. This would have been a wonderful gift in itself, but, to make it even more special, my friend had inserted my name into each of the verses so that, when I read each verse, it was as if God were speaking directly to me. As if he were calling out to Tracie by name, with his individual promises of hope, love, compassion, and peace.

Sitting quietly on my bed, away from the eyes of my husband and little ones, I allowed the tears that I had been holding in ever so tightly to escape. After the first tear fell, many followed suit. I sobbed for a few minutes into my pillow, feeling lost, hopeless, and all alone. Until God prompted me to invite him into the situation.

Snuggled in God's Lap

For lack of knowing what else to do, I wiped my eyes and placed the box gently on the bedspread. I carefully untied the yellow bow, removed the fragile lid, and slowly began to unfold each little slip of paper. As I read each verse silently, I began asking God to hear my prayers, comfort me, take away my hurt, and show me the way.

I again felt like Hannah. She and I were apparently becoming close at heart. I thought about how her desperate plea to God was worded perfectly for my situation, especially as it is translated in *The Message* Bible:

"Oh, GOD-of-the-Angel-Armies, If you'll take a good, hard look at my pain, If you'll quit neglecting me and go into action for me" (1 Samuel 1:11).

Hannah's words echoed the emotions that were bubbling in my heart like boiling water at peak temperature. I wanted God to see me sitting in my bedroom all alone with red eyes and a broken heart. I wanted him to quit neglecting me and my husband. I wanted him to take some action and do something for goodness sake! I knew he had the power, so why had he not intervened? Why was he allowing this suffering to come upon us? Ashamedly, I began to doubt his ways, as my emotional exhaustion permeated my soul.

Since I was being honest with God, I felt this was the prime opportunity to remind him that, although I wasn't perfect by any means, I was trying to live a life that would glorify him. I did try to be a good Christian, a good wife, a good mother, and a good follower of his Word. I had followed his call to become a speaker and a writer. I had made sacrifices to carry out his will for my life. So why couldn't he just make this all better? In fact, why didn't he prevent this situation from happening altogether? Why would he allow me to come under this level of stress again?

And friends, I'm just going to be honest with you. I was mad at God for not protecting me and for not keeping his hand on my marriage. I was frustrated with him for not answering my prayers. I was irritated that he had not changed my husband the way I had asked him to and ashamed at some of my own inadequacies. If you have ever felt so frustrated with God's seeming lack of concern for your most heart-wrenching problems, I know you can relate.

As I continued to sit there on my crumpled covers, my deepest thoughts, hurts, anger, and fears shoved their way to the surface with torrential force, and I could no longer hold it all in. My body slumped and I fell into a deep state of intense prayer and focus. Just like Hannah, I had nothing left to give and nothing left to do except pray and seek God's presence with my whole heart. I was weak and I knew I needed his strength to go on.

After what seemed like an eternity in silent, fervent prayer, God entered the room. I felt him move in my spirit, and his presence hovered around me. Spiritual chill bumps covered my body from head to toe. Although my eyes could not see him, my heart knew he was there. I could sense him wrapping his big, fatherly, comforting arms around me and pulling me into his presence. And you know what? I really needed a hug right then.

But he didn't stop there. He began whispering to my heart as I sat there in acute awareness of the presence of God. Then, suddenly, an idea popped into my mind that could have come only from God. I would have never thought of doing something quite this bizarre on my own accord.

God's quiet whisper said, *Tracie, lay the verses from the box all around you. Trust me.*

I pondered that thought for a moment, thinking it sounded a little fanatical and weird. I wondered what someone would think if they came into my bedroom and saw me swimming in my bed in a bunch of little papers. I could envision the wide-eyed looks of my children if they were to pounce into my bedroom and interrupt this private moment, concluding that Mommy had finally gone off the deep end.

But in a split second, God recaptured my attention and I realized that, in that moment with him, nothing else mattered but him. My spirit quickened and my heart began to beat faster as I felt him nudging me to obey this simple request. So, instead of glancing at a couple of verses and then putting them back into the box, as I normally did, I proceeded to take them all out and spread them around me on the bed.

I laid most of the verses directly in front of me, so my eyes could wander over the words of comfort they held, allowing his precious peace to saturate my soul as I read each one over and over. I placed several verses to my right and several to my left. Then, hesitantly, and feeling a little silly, I turned around and laid a few of them behind me, propping them up on my soggy pillow that had been used as a tear catcher just a few moments earlier. I paused and looked at what I had done.

As I sat on my bed, fully surrounded on every side by holy Words and divine promises inscribed with my name, I heard these words wash through my spirit, *Sweet child, you are now sitting in my lap.*

I was sitting in God's lap? My heart skipped a beat. The thought of it nearly took my breath away. It was only then that I realized I *was* sitting in the comforting, safe lap of my heavenly Father, who loved me enough to hold me. God *had* seen me in my bedroom and had reached down to hold me, his little girl.

What an indescribable privilege to know that God had invited me to not only sit with him but to be nestled into his holy lap. To be in the presence of the most high and sovereign God. To be hugged by the One who gave me life. The One who remembered me. The One who loved me. The One who could comfort me. The One who had never neglected me but had simply waited patiently for me to acknowledge my need for him and invite him to take control of my circumstance.

I cannot explain the astonishing peace that came over me in that moment. It was a peace that flooded my heart as I felt the power of his written promises, specifically *for* Tracie and *to* Tracie, sprinkled all around me. The weight of the stress that was suffocating me before I walked into that bedroom seemed to be lifted.

My spirit leapt as I realized that I was no longer merely surrounded by typed slips of paper; I was surrounded by countless reassurances that God had heard my prayers. He was not neglecting me, nor had he forgotten me. In fact, he was sitting on the bed with me, holding my heart and catching every tear, just as we are told he does in Psalm 56:8: "You keep track of all my sorrows. You have collected all my tears in your bottle. You have recorded each one in your book."

God embraced this opportunity, when the wounds of my heart were bleeding profusely, to gently and lovingly remind me that he cared me enough to show himself in a way that I could feel and understand. He loved me enough to bring me peace. All I had to do was say those two little words that he loved to hear, *"Yes, Lord,"* and accept the gift he was offering.

After that life-changing encounter with God, I knew I had to let go of the steering wheel of my marriage and allow God to take over. I had to stop trying to change my husband and ask God to change me first. I had to quit trying to fix our relationship and allow God to do his repair work in both of us. I had to relinquish my hurt and ask for strength to forgive. I had to lay my marriage and my emotions at God's feet so that he could carry the burden for me—pulling my husband and me both closer to him.

I released my pain into the hands of the only One who has the power to heal all things, including relationships. I put my full trust in him. I agreed to wait, no matter how long it took, to see how he would work.

As I thought about these things, the tears began to flow again. But this time, they were tears of relief and gratitude and joy . . . but, most of all, peace.

I had entered into a holy place when I walked into the confines of my bedroom, and I walked out a new person. I vowed to trust God's ways, even if I did not understand them or like them. I had to be willing to wait for God's best even though the waiting period would be difficult.

The difference between this waiting period and the wait that I had already been enduring was that I was no longer *hoping* that he would see me, *wishing* that he would work, or *wondering* if he would care. Instead, I *knew* that he would be at work in my marriage, and that somehow, some-way, someday he would be glorified through our sufferings.

My marriage circumstances did not change that day, and my relationship with my husband did not improve overnight. But over time, and through incredible divine interventions that God has orchestrated since then, the commitment between me and my husband is strong and secure. Although we have had to work through a lot of hard stuff, we have both grown closer to God and more in love with each other than ever before. And this love was worth the wait.

Our Flawless Role Model

Everyone experiences stress, even Jesus did. However, when we look at the abundant life that he led as he walked on earth as a man, we see that Jesus was never in a hurry. He was never worried about his reputation or the gossip or slander that people were saying behind his back. I cannot recall any situations in the Bible when Jesus seemed frazzled or disheveled, running around frantically trying to get everything done on his daily to-do lists. And when he did have to deal with people in conflict situations, he handled them with love, gentleness, self-control, and patience. Even in his anger, he did not sin. First Peter 2:21–24 offers a glimpse of how Jesus handled himself in a time of excessive stress:

> For God called you to do good, even if it means suffering, just as Christ suffered for you. He is your example, and you must follow in his steps. He never sinned, nor ever deceived anyone. He did not retaliate when he was insulted, nor threaten revenge when he suffered. He left his case in the hands of God, who always judges fairly. He personally carried our sins in his body on the cross so that we can be dead to sin and live for what is right. By his wounds you are healed.

Jesus suffered at the hands of others, yet he did not sin. He suffered without being filled with thoughts of revenge and retaliation. He suffered without pointing fingers. He even prayed for his enemies, including those who were mercilessly persecuting him. He suffered without questioning the reason why he had to suffer.

Despite his pain, Jesus knew that if it was happening, it was the will of his Father. So, even at his lowest point, he willingly took on the punishment of the world with gentleness and grace.

Hebrews 2:18 tells us that because he physically experienced what we go through on this earth, he is able to come to our rescue when we are feeling like we can't take anymore: "Since he himself has gone through suffering and testing, he is able to help us when we are being tested." The New International Version Bible translates it this way: "Because he himself suffered when he was tempted, he is able to help those who are being tempted." No one is immune to the temptation of worry and stress—they are a fact of life and a test of our faith. Although Jesus would prefer that we trust him fully in all things, he understands our weaknesses and is available to help us persevere.

In my case, however, I seem to handle suffering a little less gracefully than Jesus. There are countless days when I find myself frazzled, disheveled, and worried. Unfortunately, on these days when I am stressed and distressed, those adjectives describing Jesus' behavior are not words that would typically describe me. My normal way of handling stressful circumstances would not be characterized by love, calmness, self-control, or patience. Even after many years of praying to God for a sweet and gentle spirit, stress can still bring out the worst in me!

The truth is, no matter how strong we think our faith is, we can never live up to the standards and perfection of Jesus. We will never be able to handle stress with holiness as he did. We will never be immune to the temptations of reacting to stress in negative ways, but we can rest in knowing that Jesus understands our shortcomings. Lamentations 3:23 reassures us that his mercies are renewed every morning. He knows that we can never be just like him, but he encourages each of us to give it our best shot by following his lead.

Bear in mind, however, as we strive to carry out the will of God, that we should be focused on *being* Christians, not just looking like them. It is not simply our belief in Jesus that equips us to follow his example. The Bible says in James 2:19 that even the devil believes: "You believe that there is one God. Good! Even the demons believe that—and shudder" (NIV). Instead, it is the genuine love for him in our hearts that compels us to follow his lead. If our hearts are not in the right place, the amount of time we spend trying to do all the right things will be pointless.

We could actually be at church every time the door opens and still be completely separated and disconnected from God. I once heard Joyce Meyer, a popular television evangelist, say that we could spend all day long sitting in a garage, but that would never make us turn into a car. I love that quote—it is so true! Going to church does not make someone a Christian; it is instead meant to be a resource for increasing our faith through worship and communion with other believers. In the same way, we can believe that every word in the Bible is flawless and still not allow it to shape our lives or impact our thoughts and behaviors (or our stress levels).

I recently participated in a Bible study written by Beth Moore called *Mercy Triumphs*—an in-depth, and might I say incredible, study of James, the half brother of Jesus. I drank in every word of this powerful study, and, as God would have it, I was going through some difficult adversities at the time and needed the profound encouragement that I gleaned from this study. It is a wonderful resource for anyone going through hard times, but there was one particular paragraph that really touched my heart, discussing the importance of being connected with God and his Word.

> We can underline our Bibles till our pens run dry without a drop of ink splattering our lives. The self-deception slithers in when we mistake appreciation for application or being touched with being changed. The Word of God is meant to do more than penetrate. It's meant to activate. It can bore holes through obstacles. It can tumble defenses. It can plant wandering feet of clay in places of divine purpose. It can sanctify the sin sick and steady the aimless and confused. It can light a blazing torch in a black hole. Simply put, the Word was meant to work. And, through it, we were meant to bear fruit.[19]

Our behaviors, actions, and service to God should be an outward extension of our inward beliefs, but that is not always the case. I heard a story recently about an elderly lady in my home church who had served in our congregation for dozens of years. One Sunday, in the midst of a powerful sermon, God broke through her mask and penetrated her heart for the very first time. She realized that she had never really accepted Jesus as her personal Savior but had only been going through the motions of being a "good Christian." She was physically engaged but spiritually disconnected from the Jesus she was worshipping.

It is often this invisible disconnection, the fact that we have been deceiving ourselves about our core beliefs, that prevents us from being able to manifest the patient and peaceful character traits of God when we are faced with major stressors.

Being a Christian not only means serving God with our bodies but serving him with our hearts, souls, and minds. It means being totally sold-out to Christ in all aspects of our lives—surrendering all of our thoughts and actions to him. It means seeking the Lord with such great intensity that everything else pales in comparison. In turn, it is this intensity that helps us to be keenly aware of our need for his help to deal with our stress in the most effective ways. Once we are fully connected with Jesus, we will begin craving an insatiable daily portion of him to nourish our souls and fill our spirits with the peace we are starving for.

Craving a Daily Portion

If the phrase "you are what you eat" were literally true, my son would be a bowl of chocolate ice cream. Before he was even old enough to say "ice cream," he loved it—but only chocolate.

Once when little Michael was four years old, he pleaded in his sweet little-boy voice for some chocolate ice cream. "Pleeeaaassseeeee, Mommy," he said with blue eyes bulging and bottom lip poked out for sympathy's sake. I could never say no to such an adorable face (and he was fully aware of my weakness), so I agreed and pulled the gallon of ice cream out of the freezer. I pried open the lid and realized it was nearly empty, so rather than exhaust my arm muscles trying to scoop and scoop and scoop to get that little bit of hard ice cream out, I told Michael to just get a spoon and eat it straight out of the gallon. I created a monster that day.

Once he discovered that eating out of the gallon meant that his portion would not be limited to the few scoops I put into a bowl, life changed as he knew it. Never again did he ask for ice cream without taking a shot at proposing that he eat out of the gallon.

I can't help but smile every time he asks me that question now, because it has become a running joke between us. That boy loves him some chocolate ice cream and simply never wants his portion to be limited.

In the same way, we should never want our portion of God to be limited. If we are spiritually connected to God, we will have a hunger for him that can never be satisfied—always longing for more of his Word and possessing a desire for unlimited portions. Psalm 73:26 says, "My flesh and my heart may fail, but God is the strength of my heart and my portion forever" (NIV).

This verse refers to "portion" to describe that, although we will fail, God is enough to make up for our human-ness. God offers us the exact portion of him that we need to get through life—if we are hungry enough to ask for it and seek it out. What a blessing it is to know that we can "eat out of the gallon" every day when it comes to getting a good portion of God (with the advantage of not having to worry about calories).

We all need a portion of his peace every day, and it can be ours if we stay plugged into the One who is dishing it out.

Reflection Questions

1. What childhood memories come to mind that bring back feelings of peace and joy? How can you tap into those feelings of positive times to help you cope during difficult times?

What memories come to mind that conjure up feelings of stress or anxiety? If there are stressful memories that are possibly keeping you from embracing peace and joy in Christ, take a moment to talk them over with God. Ask him to help you forget the past and focus on all the good things he has for your future. Write out a heartfelt prayer asking for his clarity in understanding why you are allowing these issues to be a part of your life and to help you let the past be the past—forgiven and forgotten.

2. How are you like Hannah in the Bible? In what ways can her trust and devotion to God be motivation for you to reach out to God with your most difficult problems or deepest unmet desires?

3. Circle any of the physical problems below that you have experienced lately.

Fatigue   Headache   Upset stomach   Muscle tension
Teeth grinding   Change in sex drive   Dizziness
Irritability   Anger   Nervousness   Lack of energy
Quick to cry   Change in appetite   Unexplained health issues

Consider if any of the problems you circled could possibly be stress related. What changes can you implement in your life today to reduce your stress for the sake of improving your health?

Write your suggested areas of change on a note card and hang it on your mirror, refrigerator or anywhere you will take notice of it each day to remind you of your commitment to yourself and your health.

4. . Have you been feeling like God is absent lately? Are you just going through the motions, instead of really worshipping him? Is it possible that you have been disconnected or unplugged from God? What can you do to plug into God?

5. Write a brief prayer below about an issue you have been asking for God's help on for a long time but God has yet to answer. Then write a promise to God that you will trust him and his timing.

Prayer:

Commitment Promise:

6. Do you believe that your life would improve if you developed an insatiable craving for a portion of God's Word every day? What are three steps you can take toward this goal? How do you think meeting these goals will impact your faith level and your relationship with Christ?

7. How do you normally handle stressful situations? Is it possible that your reactions to stress could be causing additional problems in your relationships and life in general? Write down three improvements you would like to make with regards to how you react to stressful situations.

Stress Busting Scriptures

For in Christ lives all the fullness of God in a human body. So you also are complete through your union with Christ, who is the head over every ruler and authority.

Colossians 2:9–10

꩜

For we are God's masterpiece. He has created us anew in Christ Jesus, so we can do the good things he planned for us long ago.

Ephesians 2:10

꩜

Hatred stirs up quarrels, but love makes up for all offenses.

Proverbs 10:12

꩜

The LORD replied, "My Presence will go with you, and I will give you rest."

Exodus 33:14 NIV

꩜

Trust in the LORD and do good. Then you will live safely in the land and prosper. Take delight in the LORD, and he will give you your heart's desires. Commit everything you do to the LORD. Trust him, and he will help you.

Psalm 37:3–5

꩜

Bonus:
✍ Quiet Time Activity ✍

Could you use some snuggle time in God's lap? Would you like to spend some time sitting in the middle of God's Word? Below is a list of Bible verses that were included in my blessings box from my friend LeAnn, which blessed me with the opportunity to sit in God's lap.

In order to make your own blessings box, type each Bible verse into a document, and insert your name into each one. You may also want to include any verses that are special to your heart as well, and consider creating a paraphrased version in which you can insert your name in a personal way. Then print out the verses and individually cut them apart. You can put the verses in a dainty bowl, a beautiful glass box, or a paper cup—what's important is that you have them available.

Find a quiet place to spend some time with God, and strategically place the verses all around you. You could retreat to your bedroom as I did or any place that provides privacy and solace. Invite God into your heart and into your life, opening the door for him to make his presence known to you. Focus on talking with him in prayer as if he were sitting right in front of you, while remembering that as soon as you invite him in, he will be there with you.

(<u>Your name here</u>), I carry your burdens every day. Psalm 68:19

You can know and depend on the love that I have for you, (＿＿＿＿). 1 John 4:16

You can trust in my faithfulness, (＿＿＿＿), because my Word is true. Psalm 33:4

If you enter in my rest, (＿＿＿＿), you will find rest from all your striving. Hebrews 4:9–10

My Spirit will help you in your weakness, (＿＿＿＿). Romans 8:26

You can rest in my love, (_____), for I have power to save you. Zephaniah 3:17

I will meet your every need, (_____), through my eternal riches in Jesus Christ. Philippians 4:19

I will be the voice behind you, (_____), guiding you in the way you should go. Isaiah 30:21

(_____), I will give you power to know the vastness of my immeasurable love. Ephesians 3:17–19

Trust in me with all your heart, (_____), and I will guide you. Proverbs 3:5–6

Come close to me, (_____), and I will come close to you. James 4:8

I prepared a kingdom inheritance for you, (_____), when I created the world. Matthew 25:34

I am with you, (_____), and I will help you because I am your God. Isaiah 41:10

My promise of life is for you and for your family, (_____). Acts 2:39

Reach out and you will touch me, for I am not far from you, (_____). Acts 17:27

Commit all that you do to me, (_____), and your plans will be successful. Proverbs 16:3

You can trust in me, (_____), for I am your strength and your song. Isaiah 12:2

I will never abandon you, (_____). Hebrews 13:5

If you wait for me, (_____), I will work on your behalf. Isaiah 64:4

An eternal crown awaits you at the finish line, (_____). 1 Corinthians 9:24–25

I am near to you whenever you cry out, (_____). Deuteronomy 4:7

I will keep watch over you and guard you forever, (_____). Psalm 12:7

My love will never fail you, (_____). 1 Corinthians 13:8

Call on me, (_____), when you are in trouble and I will rescue you. Psalm 91:15

When problems arise, (_____), call to me and I will answer you. Psalm 86:7

The good things I have planned for you, (_____), are too many to count. Psalm 40:5

For you, (_____), are honored in my eyes. I, your God, am your strength. Isaiah 49:5

I will protect and carry you, (_____), all the days of your life. Isaiah 46:4

Though the mountains vanish, my unending love will never leave you, (_____). Isaiah 54:10

Ask me for wisdom, (_____), and I will generously give it to you. James 1:5

(_____), I have a special plan and purpose for your life. Seek hope in me. Jeremiah 29:11

Chapter Six

I Can Do It Myself . . . or Can I?

I feel sure that all of us have heard a child say those well-known words: "I can do it all by myself!" I remember when my son was learning to tie his shoes and the frustration it caused the whole family. Regardless of how many times I showed him how to do it, he still could not master the task—but that certainly did not dampen his desire to persevere. God obviously blessed him with the gift of determination!

If we had to wait thirty minutes in the kitchen while he tried to loop his white laces, making us late for wherever it was we were headed, it was of no concern to him. Time was of no consequence, only the matter at hand.

Each time I would lean down and try to offer my help, Michael would pitch a fit and yell, "I can do it all by myself!" I would sometimes feel an anxiety attack coming on, while impatiently waiting for him to get it done.

Usually that scenario would come to an end when my patience was spent. I would eventually bend down and scoop him up against his will and carry him to the car. He would writhe his skinny little body into an unbendable stick, followed by wailing and flailing around like a crazed noodle.

He was frustrated and out of sorts, simply because he had wanted to do it himself but could not. He did not have the skills, the knowledge, the hand/eye coordination, the understanding, and the attention to detail that were necessary for tying his shoes.

In the same way, we often keep trying and trying to tackle a task, change a person's heart, transform a situation, or minimize our stress—and when we can't, we get frustrated and out of sorts, too. We might even act like a child when life is not going our way. Of course, as adults, we don't become stick figures and throw ourselves on the floor like spaghetti noodles, but we certainly have our own special ways of pitching grown-up tantrums.

The underlying reason for my frustration when I get to the breaking point of wanting to throw a tantrum is that the problem seemed like something I could handle at first. But then, come to find out, I was not equipped to handle it at all. Just like my son, I simply wanted to handle the problems myself, but I could not. Therefore, my efforts were in vain, and my energy was wasted—first on the problem and second on the tantrum.

I understand a child's frustration at times like this, because, even as an adult, I often do not want to admit my need for help either. Partly because we are all taught from a young age that we need to be independent and are sometimes even groomed to believe that asking for help is a sign of weakness or an admission of failure but also partly because we all struggle with pride and want to prove our worth in the eyes of the world.

While this mind-set of pride and independence is common in our society, it is not the mind-set of Jesus. We are reminded of this truth in John 15:4–5, which says, "Remain in me, and I will remain in you. For a branch cannot produce fruit if it is severed from the vine, and you cannot be fruitful unless you remain in me. Yes, I am the vine; you are the branches. Those who remain in me, and I in them, will produce much fruit. For apart from me you can do nothing."

Notice that Jesus was not commanding but rather inviting his disciples to remain, which means to abide in him. He promised blessings and that they'd bear much "fruit." Just as an apple can only be produced

if it stays connected to the tree branch for nourishment and li
was telling them and us that we must stay connected to him. Wil
the vital life-giving union with Christ, we can bear no fruit in our live
Not merely "fruit" through acts of service for the Lord but fruit from our
hearts. The type of fruit that blossoms into such genuine peace, joy, and
confidence despite our circumstances that it can be seen by everyone we
come in contact with.

All too often we do things in our own strength and wisdom, rather
than realizing or relenting to our need for God's help. We may try tire-
lessly to tackle a task, extend forgiveness, change a person's heart, repair a
marriage, transform a situation, or accomplish a goal—and when we can't
we get frustrated and stressed, just like a child incapable of tying his shoes.

The word "abide" means to dwell in, reside in, or continue in a particular condition or relationship. Upon accepting Jesus as our Savior, we
are invited to abide in him, and this verse encourages us as to why staying
connected in a relationship is important to our faith. As we learn to dwell
in Christ daily, we are better equipped to handle stress and adversities
and better prepared to avoid meltdowns altogether.

Just like I knew my son's limitations, God understands we need his
help as we wade through life. He understands our desire for independence
and our struggle with pride, yet if we abide in him and accept his help, he
will equip us to deal with the challenges of life.

So why do we try all other avenues first, before turning to God? Why
do we allow pride to get in the way, convincing us that "we've got this"?
Why don't we realize our limitations or stumbling blocks *before* we end
up in a throw down? The answer is because the enemy wants us to feel
discouraged and ill-equipped to handle life. He wants us to falsely believe
we can do it alone. So he puts pride in our hearts, making us think we are
capable of being self-sufficient. He feeds us lies, telling us we don't need
God. He puts rebellion in our minds, fueling the fire by reminding us that
we didn't deserve these problems and it must be all God's fault, or at least
somebody's fault. He puts hurdles in our path, causing us to become more
frustrated, disappointed, and hopeless. Then, with all of his final efforts

condemns us, making us feel like epic failures,
nfidence and self-worth.

nean old enemy works. John 10:10 says, "The
d kill and destroy." He builds us up and then
path look clear and then throws sharp stones
ir hearts with untruths and then condemns

us for believing them. He comes to steal, kill, and destroy not only our tangible possessions, but our spiritual blessings. Blessings like peace and serenity and less stress. Blessings like joy and happiness. Once he destroys our hearts and our faith, the rest is child's play.

The sooner we recognize that we need to put on the full armor of God all the time and that we cannot do anything by ourselves, the sooner we will begin to understand that our quest for less stress must be dependent on God alone.

Whether we want to admit it or not, we *need* God. Until we embrace his sovereignty and power as the only way and quit trying to do things our own way, we will be doomed to a life of frustration and stress, constantly engaged in battles we are not equipped to fight. We simply cannot do it alone.

Despite how long you may have been trying to succeed, handle adversities, deal with stress, or fix problems in your life, God still longs for you to recognize your need for him and turn to him for help and divine intervention. He knows the stumbling blocks that we encounter in life, and he never withholds forgiveness. Isaiah 1:18 says, "'Come now, let's settle this,' says the LORD.' Though your sins are like scarlet, I will make them as white as snow. Though they are red like crimson, I will make them as white as wool.'" No matter how long we have been away, how much we have sinned, or how long we have tried to do life without God, he is always waiting to shower us with the love and peace that he promised.

In this passage in John 15, Jesus was not only inviting his disciples to abide in him, but he also offered them encouragement that although they cannot do anything apart from him, they can do anything if they remained in him. He wanted them to know their need for him but also wanted to bless them with the motivation to trust him and rely on his strength in all things. He wanted them to know if they were willing to lay down their pride, be humble in spirit, and abide in him, that he would always abide in them as well. When we learn the importance of the word "abide," peace can blossom.

What stumbling blocks have you encountered lately? Doubt? Fear? Worry? Concern? Confusion? Desperation? Fatigue? Frustration? Feeling overworked? Job stressors? Overwhelmed? Marriage problems? Parenting challenges? Financial worries? Illness? The death of a loved one?

Will you admit your need for God right now? Are you ready to stop trying to drive through life full speed on your own and start giving God the wheel?

Allow him to cleanse your heart of any stumbling blocks that are preventing you from understanding his peace. Turn those situations over to him that are causing you the most stress, and do not, under any circumstance, try to take them back.

I promise you, he can handle it.

The Lion Never Sleeps

I have learned in my journey of faith that, the closer I am walking with God, the more likely the devil will be working to make me stumble.

Reality has proven that the minute we say, "*Yes,*" to God's peace and God's plans and begin to strive after a life focused on him, the devil places a big red target on our chests and starts firing off shots at our hearts.

I have experienced more than my fair share of spiritual warfare in the past few years as I have devoted my life to ministry and my relationship with Christ, but one specific example of being attacked by the enemy when I was on fire for God always comes to mind. It happened early on in my speaking ministry, after I had spoken at an out-of-town event.

After experiencing God in wonderful ways at this women's retreat and witnessing his healing power work mightily in the hearts of many, I left the event on a spiritual high. Not because of anything I had done or shared but because of what I had seen God do in the hearts of those I was ministering to. Sunday afternoon rolled around, and the time came for me to start out on my three-hour drive home.

All the way home, I listened to praise music and sang at the top of my lungs, filled with a joy that I assumed was inextinguishable. I was praising God, thanking him for the opportunity to serve him, and overflowing with gratitude for the precious family that I would soon be reunited with when I returned home. I finally pulled into my driveway with great anticipation, hopped out of the car, and scurried inside the house to begin passing out hugs and kisses to everyone.

But things did not go exactly as planned. Upon entering the house, I was abruptly faced with an acute awareness of my recent absence. As I stepped through the front door, I tripped over shoes, toys, and book bags that had apparently been there for three days from when the kids came home from school on Friday.

I then headed into the kitchen, only to find it a complete disaster of huge proportion. Plates, glasses, silverware, and used napkins were everywhere. The trash can was filled to the brim with garbage, and the sink was overflowing with stinky, yucky, dirty dishes, granting me firsthand knowledge of what my husband fed the children at every meal over the weekend.

As I went to place my suitcase in the laundry room, I was nearly attacked by a two-foot monster of soiled clothes and towels, which was eerily creeping out of the laundry room and into the hall, ready to devour anything in its path. How could three kids and one husband generate so many dirty clothes in three days?!

And that was just the downstairs. The bedrooms upstairs . . . well, let's just not go there.

As I looked in shock at what appeared to be the aftermath of a tornado, I felt a twinge of irritation begin creeping into my spirit and a hot angry knot slowly making its way into my throat. My face began to flush and my emotions erupted to the surface.

In that instant, my attitude changed from one of gratefulness, love, and anticipation, to frustration, resentment, and a flurry of anger. It was as if the devil had taken a knife and plunged it into my heart, allowing all the sweet memories of the weekend to spill out onto the floor, shattering into fragile pieces.

I can't say that my head spun around backwards, but if it were possible, it might have occurred. I suddenly began wondering why no one else in the house could clean up anything besides me?! I became obsessed with the mess.

I immediately decided that, unless my husband's arms had fallen off, rendering him incapable of picking anything up, or unless he had experienced a temporary loss of vision preventing him from seeing our home in its current state of complete chaos, I had a few words to share with him . . . and they would most definitely not be including the phrase, "I missed you, dear."

I quickly began focusing on the countless reasons why I was completely justified in being upset about the chaotic state of my household, and, unfortunately, I played right along with the evil one's game like putty in his hands.

I chose that very moment, which was meant to be a loving homecoming, to make it crystal clear to my family that I was not a happy camper. I immediately began blurting out what chores each child needed to take care of and how they each needed to be a part of the solution for this existing disaster. I also made them keenly aware of their responsibilities, which should be carried out in full when I am away traveling in the future. And then I took the opportunity to let my husband know that he seriously fell short of my expectations during my absence. It's possible that there are some drill sergeants out there who would have had more compassion than I doled out.

In less than ten minutes of arriving back home, my feelings of spiritual bliss had quickly vanished. In addition to my nerves being shot and my blood pressure hitting the roof, my family was now avoiding me like the plague!

As I stood there in the fallout of the storm I had ushered in upon opening the door, a feeling of dread began to overtake my body. I suddenly felt like a total failure and was discouraged that not only had I lost all self-control but I had also fallen into an all-too-familiar trap that the devil had carefully devised.

This was not the first time this had happened. I had come home after several mountaintop experiences only to find messy dishes, messy bedrooms, and messy children. I had fallen into that trap before, and yet once again I allowed myself to get caught. But feeling like a fool was the least of my worries now.

My heart became overwhelmingly heavy as I realized the emotional destruction that I had left behind in my wake—so my thoughts turned to beating myself up over why I allowed myself to get so upset about such trivial things. Hot tears began to pierce my eyes as my heart sunk with regret. It was only ten minutes of words, but they were words with sting.

As I meandered to my bedroom to unpack my suitcase, while everyone else was busy carrying out my recently dictated orders, I found myself crying out to God—*Oh, God! What just happened?! Just moments ago, I was on cloud nine, basking in the glory of your love—floating on a cloud of faith, anxious to embrace the ones I love most. Yet now I am consumed with feelings of frustration and disappointment in myself, while my family is suffering the consequences of my ugly outbursts! What is wrong with me?*

In a pit of discouragement and shame, still wondering what kind of mother would fuss at her adorable little children whom she hadn't seen in three days and what kind of wife would make her husband feel completely inferior after having been a single parent all weekend, I decided to put myself in a grown-up timeout and spend some time with God.

As I prayed, asking for forgiveness, wisdom, and strength, it all suddenly became crystal clear. Upon leaving such a powerful weekend-worship experience, I had become imminent prey for the devil. He wanted me to be stressed so I would take my eyes off of God, so I was on his hit list, and he had taken aim, fired, and hit his target.

Fortunately, he merely brought me down to my knees. Knees that bowed in humility to an almighty God whose love and forgiveness overpowered even the most evil attempts of the fallen one.

First Peter 5:8 warns, "Stay alert! Watch out for your great enemy, the devil. He prowls around like a roaring lion, looking for someone to devour." The enemy had been prowling around like a lion, trying to figure out when and how to devour the joy and fulfillment I had been saturated with over the weekend. He was lurking around the corner, watching me, waiting to pounce and devour my spirit at the first opportunity. And he pounced with a fierce presence, using everyday obstacles that he knew would make me stumble and fall. He wanted to make sure I didn't infect anyone with my peace and joy.

My heart had been quickly transformed from a heart on fire for God to a heart dealing with petty situations that tested my patience and my love walk. And because of fatigue and frustration, I had given the devil a temporary foothold. Ephesians 4:27 tells us that we should "not give the devil a foothold" (NIV). I had not only given the devil a foothold that day, I flung the door wide open and invited him in!

After God cleaned up that mess in my heart, I gathered my family together to clean up the mess I had inflicted upon their little hearts (which caused the messiness in my house to pale in comparison). Then the homecoming I had envisioned began to unfold, and we snuggled on the couch for the rest of night with some much needed popcorn-and-a-movie therapy.

That day was an eye-opening experience and serves as a vivid reminder of how sneaky and conniving the devil really is. It also reminds me that stumbling blocks to our faith, and our peace, are not always huge dramatic circumstances. Sometimes they may be nothing more than a sink full of dirty dishes and a pile of dirty laundry.

At times the little things in life can be more stressful than the big. So we must carefully guard our hearts so as not to become obsessed with the mess of life, because the thief loves making the most of a mess.

Prepare for the Thief

John 10:10a says, "The thief comes only to steal and kill and destroy" (NIV).

There are people who doubt the existence of Satan—people who wonder how an angel could fall from grace and why God would allow that to happen, people who think the whole concept of heaven and hell is farfetched and don't believe that God, who is supposed to love everyone, would allow such a horrific place to exist.

Maybe you are one of those people, and maybe you are not; but I want to take this opportunity to address some of the concerns that I often hear. Although I do not claim to be a Bible scholar, I do boldly claim to be a Bible believer, and the Bible says that Satan is real and active. The primary way we can feel confident in the existence of the devil is that the Lord Jesus Christ himself recognized him as such.

In Luke 10:18 Jesus said, "I saw Satan fall from heaven like lightning!" In Matthew 4:10, when Satan approached Jesus in the wilderness to tempt him, Jesus exclaimed, "Get out of here, Satan. . . . For the Scriptures say, 'You must worship the LORD your God and serve only him.'" And John 14:30 portrays Jesus calling the devil what he really is: "I don't have much more time to talk to you, because the ruler of this world approaches. He has no power over me." The NIV Bible translates this verse to say "the prince of this world."

The Apostles Paul and John both referred to the devil on more than one occasion, calling him names like "the god of this world" in 2 Corinthians 4:4, "the commander of the powers in the unseen world" in Ephesians 2:2, and "the evil one" in 1 John 5:19. Revelation 12:9 gives a true picture of him—the deceiver—when it says, "This great dragon—the ancient serpent called the devil, or Satan, the one deceiving the whole world—was thrown down to the earth with all his angels."

The second piece of evidence that should convince us of the existence of the devil is when we see him working in our lives and in our world. We see his evil schemes being carried out by people in our society every day. In fact, sometimes I am left paralyzed in shock and despair when I watch the news and hear of horrible acts of evil taking place all over the world. The devil is real, and he is actively pursuing his goal for power over our hearts and power over this world.

Let us never forget that he is not a fictitious character, wearing a red suit with a pointed tail, spiked horns, and carrying a pitchfork. He is real, and his sole purpose is to cause us to stumble and fall by filling our lives with stress and worry. But in John 10:10b Jesus says, "My purpose is to give them a rich and satisfying life." The NIV Bible translates it, "I have come that they may have life, and have it to the full." And the ESV Bible puts it this way: "I came that they may have life and have it abundantly." That full, rich, satisfying, and abundant life—a life with less stress and more peace—is ours for the asking, yet we must never forget that the lion is lurking.

Just like a lion looking for something or someone to devour in order to satisfy its selfish hunger for destruction, the devil's influence on our hearts can be relentless and deadly. The funny thing about lions is that they are actually beautiful and majestic creatures to look at, unlike the mental picture we have of Satan. Lions give off the appearance of royalty, calmness, and strength, so, as we peer at them behind the safety of glass, we often forget that lions are not only physically strong and powerful but they are very patient predators. They make their living out of quietly waiting in the shadows until just the right moment, when their victim is unaware of the danger and therefore most vulnerable to attack.

After that unfortunate day when my homecoming was tainted because of the lurking lion, I made a personal commitment to always be aware of what is going on around me and recognize when the enemy is at work, patiently waiting to attack during my most vulnerable moments—not just when I arrive home after being out of town but in my everyday life.

I made a mental note that in the future, no matter what the house looks like when I return home from traveling, I would exhibit nothing but love to my family and gratitude to my Jesus for taking care of them while I was away. I asked God to help me be blinded to any obstacles that may fight for my attention when I open the front door and to see nothing except the gleaming faces of those precious family members who are so happy that I have returned home. And, most importantly, I asked God to prick my spirit with awareness when the lion is crouching in other areas of my life.

We would never ask for a life of stress and worry, but, by ignoring the reality that the devil is lurking, we are actually throwing in the towel and surrendering to such a life. It is our choice who will have dominion over our lives—the evil one or the Holy One.

The lion never tires of his evil ways, but we can have great peace in knowing that our God never slumbers. Psalm 121:4 reads, "indeed, he who watches over Israel will neither slumber nor sleep" (NIV).

Prepped for Battle

If we consistently prepare and equip ourselves for battle, even when no battle seems to exist, then we will be ready to fight back when the battle does begin. A soldier cannot wait until a battle begins to load his gun and practice his aim; instead, he has to prepare ahead of time so that, when the strike happens, he is ready to strike back. The same goes for us in our own lives. We have to be ready for the war that is being waged against our hearts each and every day by staying connected to our Savior.

Each of us has different circumstances, problems, challenges, and stressors, but if we really think about it, our inability to overcome those stumbling blocks often derives from one major problem: pride.

My tarnished homecoming was a prime example of not only a lurking enemy but also a prideful heart. My pride told me that I should not have to clean up a messy house that I wasn't even around to dirty. After all, I had been doing ministry. I had been called to do something for the kingdom of God, and everyone else should appreciate that and at least take care of the house while I am away doing my wonderful service for the Lord. My pride told me that my husband should meet my standards of parenting and housekeeping and that he should step fully into my shoes when I am away. And, when he didn't, my pride told me that I should let him know how he failed. My inward pride became an outward mess, and I had to seek God's strength to focus on him, not on myself or my personal feelings of righteousness. Scripture makes it clear that God despises the prideful man:

> Fear of the LORD is the foundation of true knowledge,
> but fools despise wisdom and discipline. (Prov. 1:7)

Don't be impressed with your own wisdom.
Instead, fear the LORD and turn away from evil. (Prov. 3:7)

All who fear the LORD will hate evil.
Therefore, I hate pride and arrogance,
corruption and perverse speech. (Prov. 8:13)

Pride goes before destruction,
and haughtiness before a fall. (Prov. 16:18)

During my years of working full time in a corporate office, I witnessed so many people living lives full of pride, arrogance, and self-superiority only to plunge quickly into a sea of despair, embarrassment, and regret when corporate decisions didn't go their way. People who became overly confident with their own self-value, only to find themselves feeling inferior and lost when their circumstances changed or spun out of their control. Yet pride doesn't only happen in the workplace; if we aren't careful, it can weave its sticky tentacles into every part of our lives, wreaking havoc and destroying relationships at every turn.

Pride is a tool of the devil used to feed our egos, making us think that we really are bigger and better than others and that we don't need anyone else but ourselves, not even God. Prideful people may not come right out and say they don't need God, but their attitude about their self-worth and their personal importance speaks loud and clear.

Maybe you do not think this section is relevant to you. Maybe you are a very humble person and feel as if you don't struggle with pride at all. But pride is not always self-promoting. Sometimes it can be self-degrading as well. Consider this thought: Do you ever assume that people wouldn't want to spend time with you or care about your opinions or your problems, because you are not good enough or because you probably don't meet their standards of importance? Do you wonder if God could ever really love someone like you? Do you tend to put yourself down frequently or have difficulty accepting a compliment?

Is it possible that the reason you feel as if God doesn't see you or your problems or care about your stress is because you are focused on you, instead of God? Have you been throwing your own pity parties and forgetting to invite God in because you assume he wouldn't want to spend time with someone like you?

Even if your heart is not full of self-worth but instead full of self-doubt, that is still a form of pride. Pride is a complicated feeling and a tricky game of emotions, and, unfortunately, the devil knows every way to play the game.

Pride is not only giving ourselves too much credit for the good things in our lives but also giving ourselves a lack of credit for anything. If we see ourselves as superior to others, then we take the focus away from God and put it on us. On the other hand, if we see ourselves as worthless and inferior, then we take the focus away from God and put it on us again.

God not only sees our flaws, mistakes, and insecurities, he loves us despite them. He sees a deeper beauty and worth in us than what anyone else can see, even more than what we see in the mirror every day.

He not only sees our circumstances, he considers them. He ponders them. He chooses whether, how, and when he is going to intervene. Sometimes his intervention solves our problems, and sometimes he equips us to deal with the stress and heartache that those problems bring. Psalm 10:14 says, "But you see the trouble and grief they cause. You take note of it and punish them. The helpless put their trust in you. You defend the orphans."

A great test of faith is when we begin to look beyond ourselves and beyond pride and instead into the eyes of Christ, trusting that he is there and working, even when we can't see him.

You may still be wondering why the discussion of pride is relevant to a book on stress. Well, simply put, pride in any form will eventually lead to stress. It is a condition that makes the heart sick. And when the heart is sick, we are ill-prepared to deal with the stressors of life.

Once we admit our pride in either form and humble ourselves enough to admit that we are not equipped or capable of handling anything without God, only then we will begin traveling down the road that leads to a life fully entrusted to him. A life where we let go of the reins and give God complete sovereignty over our future.

God cannot mend our hearts if we never admit they are broken. If we fail to recognize our inability to overcome our greatest challenges by ourselves, we will never feel led to seek out God. We may even unintentionally become passive in our relationship with him, putting him on the back burner. But just because we stop looking for God does not mean he has taken a break from looking for us. Instead, we are simply not seeing him, because we are only seeing ourselves—either in our magnified self-worth or our magnified lack of self-worth. In either circumstance, we are discounting God's authority over our lives.

Rebel and Suffer the Consequences

"Rebel" is an ugly word. It's most commonly used in reference to teenagers who try to buck every rule their parents set, but if we have ever complained, grumbled, or whined about a situation in our lives, then we have rebelled in the same exact way. Complaining is nothing more than grumbling in our hearts against God. It is assuming that we know better than God (there goes that pride problem again) and that he is not handling the situation as we would like.

What it boils down to is that complaining is simply the act of not trusting God's sovereignty—assuming that if he would answer our prayers in the ways we have asked or if he would just follow the outline that we gave him for finding a resolution, then all would be well.

Remember when I said in Chapter One that most of our stress comes from trying to control things that we have no control over? It is so true! How many days or nights have you spent on your knees, desperately crying out to God, laying out your ideas for how he should fix a problem in your life, and getting more and more frustrated each day when you don't see him working the way you want? Unfortunately, many people get so tired of waiting that they try to do what they want, despite God's rules. That is rebelling against God. Just like a teenager who is grounded for his choices, our rebellion can result in consequences as well.

One summer when my son was nine years old, he wanted to play outside in the water sprinkler. It was a typical, hot, July day in the South, which certainly warranted a romp in the cool water. However, I could only assume that my neighbor would not appreciate her son, who was playing at my house at the time, coming home for dinner dripping wet.

So, despite his pleading request, I told him that we would save the sprinkler for another day. Michael didn't like that answer and tried to coerce me to change my mind, but, upon seeing that I wouldn't budge on my answer, he finally said okay and skipped off back outside.

About thirty minutes later, he came inside to get a drink. I noticed he was either sweating profusely or soaking wet. I said, "Michael, why are you so wet?" His eyes glazed over, as if he actually thought I would not notice the water cascading from his hair and clothing. He then proceeded to tell me how they had played in the sprinkler . . . but just for a few minutes.

I asked him why he did that after I had told him not to, and his only answer was, "But we *really* wanted to."

He seemed to think that since he only rebelled for "just a few minutes" and since it was something that he thought would bring great pleasure his actions were justified. He erroneously believed that since he *really* wanted to do it his decisions and plans were surely best and definitely more important than the instruction he had been given. He quickly learned that he was mistaken on both counts.

It would be easy to excuse that type of rebellion by blaming it on the lack of good judgment of a child, but, in all honesty, don't we, as adults, do that same thing with God? We ask God for something, but if he doesn't answer our prayers the way we want, we go off on our own and try to make that "something" happen, even if for "just a few minutes." But time is of no essence to God; obedience is everything. Or, we may just go with our desires because we *really* wanted to, but our God is also not One to fall for lame excuses any more than a smart mom is.

Just like my son wanted to disobey for only a short time, following his own agenda, which he thought was worth the risk, we too can get ourselves in trouble when we try to answer our own prayers, coerce God into agreeing with us, or follow our feelings instead of our faith when God says no or not now. The end result leaves us dripping wet and guilty as charged with the consequences close at hand.

The truth is, we can whine and complain all we want to God, but he still may not say yes. We may tire of waiting on him to agree or answer the way we would like, but that does not make our disobedience any more acceptable. We may think we know better than he does, but choosing our ways over his is nothing but mockery.

Galatians 6:7–8 says, "Don't be misled—you cannot mock the justice of God. You will always harvest what you plant. Those who live only to satisfy their own sinful nature will harvest decay and death from that sinful nature. But those who live to please the Spirit will harvest everlasting life from the Spirit."

We may try to fix the problems in the way we feel is most suitable, while feeling perfectly capable and justified in doing so. However, if our self-imposed solution is outside of God's will, the road we have chosen will not be a smooth one.

Life is sometimes a bumpy, and often painful, journey as a result of trying to be god over our lives. Yet just like that rebellious teenager who misses curfew, or a little boy who simply wants to get wet on a hot summer day, there are consequences for our rebellion too—and those consequences may cause more stress than we bargained for.

Are you beginning to see a pattern here? A pattern proving that, every time we turn from God and forget that he desires to rule over our hearts and decisions, the end result is always more stress?

✍ Reflection Questions

1. What does "abiding in Christ" mean to you? Consider looking up several definitions of the word "abide," and ask yourself whether the definitions define your walk with Christ. Ponder ways you can begin to truly abide in Christ, and write them down here.

2. What problem or burden have you been trying to handle all by yourself, apart from God? How is that working out for you? What positive things might occur if you turned this problem over to God?

3. What stumbling blocks has the devil thrown in your path lately? Are there any people or situations in your life that consistently cause you to stumble? How can you equip yourself to be better prepared going forward? (Remember we may not be able to change our circumstances, but we can change our reactions toward them through Christ working within us.)

4. Do you struggle to believe that there is an enemy working against the world? If applicable, who or what has influenced your opinion to believe that the Bible sheds inaccurate information about the existence of the devil?

5. Do you believe God's Word is true, yet sometimes struggle to believe that there are forces of evil working against us in this world?

If this is an area you struggle with, how can you increase your awareness of when you are in a "spiritual battle"?

6. Does self-boasting or self-loathing pride exist in your heart? Is this pride creating a barrier between you and God and allowing or causing further stress to come into your life? Write a prayer of honest humility to God, confessing your pride in any form and asking for the ability to embrace your self-worth in him alone.

7. Is there anything God asked you to do in the past that you ignored because you thought your plan was better? What did you learn about trusting God and waiting on his ways and his timing?

Stress Busting Scriptures

I can do everything through him who gives me strength.

Philippians 4:13 NIV

But seek first his kingdom and his righteousness,
and all these things will be given to you as well.

Matthew 6:33 NIV

If you obey my commands, you will remain in my love,
just as I have obeyed my Father's commands and remain in his love.

John 15:10 NIV

For everything in the world—the cravings of sinful man, the lust of his eyes
and the boasting of what he has and does—comes not from the
Father but from the world.

1 John 2:16 NIV

For our struggle is not against flesh and blood, but against the rulers,
against the authorities, against the powers of this dark world
and against the spiritual forces of evil in the heavenly realms.

Ephesians 6:12 NIV

Chapter Seven

Overcoming Your Giants

Our problems and our stress can sometimes seem so much bigger than we can handle, especially when we are not only facing one giant problem but many. You may be facing a major giant right now—being in a personal relationship that has suffered many blows, a marriage that is crumbling more and more every day, a spouse addicted to pornography, a friend or family member held hostage by substance abuse, an inability to find employment despite daily efforts for months, home foreclosure, difficult bosses, harassing credit and collection phone calls, tragic accidents, chronic or terminal illness, family problems, abuse, or worse.

Sometimes even our greatest efforts to manage our stress can seem futile when our giants seem too huge to ever overcome. Instead of seeing progress, we feel like we are just beating our head against the wall, over and over, becoming more stressed-out as the reality sinks in that we cannot change the situations that are stressing us, no matter how badly we wish we could.

Ever been there? I know I have. I used to wake up every morning and start thinking about all the yucky things that I had to face that day. I would try to give myself a pep talk to pre-empt negativity: *Today I will not allow things, circumstances, or people to push me over the edge. No matter what, I commit to maintaining my temper, my poise, and my attitude. I will trust God to be my portion and walk in his ways.* However, within two hours that heart-felt commitment would become a distant memory as I jumped headfirst into the day and got sucked deeper and deeper into all of my problems. In fact, on some days, it actually seemed like life had a chokehold on me, and, no matter what I did, I couldn't pry its ugly fingers from around my weakened jugular.

By the grace of God alone, I feel so blessed to have discovered years ago that life does not have to be that way and that God never intended for it to be. He never intended for us to lead lives of despair, stress, and dread. He never meant for us to be so bogged down with worry and stress that we would dread getting up in the morning, although this type of living became a reality when sin came into his perfect world. But God is still God. We cannot escape our lives, but he is our escape from stress.

Overcoming your stress begins with recognizing the fact that, no matter what problems are causing you stress and anxiety, God IS BIGGER. Yes, he is bigger than the issue you are thinking about right now. He is bigger than the hopelessness that seems to be engulfing your every breath. He is bigger than the greatest fears you hold in your heart. He is bigger than the unrelenting stress that plagues your heart as you try to juggle all the demands for your time and attention throughout the day. He is bigger than your biggest challenge, whatever it may be.

In *Prince Caspian*, from the popular Chronicles of Narnia series, C. S. Lewis tells the story of children on a fictional adventure, sprinkling in countless spiritual lessons throughout the book. In this book a little girl named Lucy encounters Aslan, the gentle lion who portrays the Christ-figure in the Narnia stories. Lucy loved Aslan, as did everyone, including me and my children. By this point in the story, when Lucy comes upon Aslan, it had been a while since she had seen him. So, upon encountering him, they had this very brief yet thought provoking conversation:

"Aslan," said Lucy, "you're bigger."

"That is because you are older, little one," answered he.

"Not because you are?"

"I am not. But every year you grow, you will find me bigger."[20]

As we become more mature in faith, learning to trust that God is capable of all things, we will see God as bigger and bigger every time we encounter him. God is and was and always will be the same, but, as we give him sovereignty over our hearts, our awe of him increases.

Each time he intervenes in our lives, we witness his power, and our view of him grows. Once we allow ourselves to grasp how big God really is, we can learn to put aside worry and rest in knowing that he can handle our problems—leaving no need for us to destroy ourselves stressing over them.

One of the biggest mistakes that Christians make is seeing the giants in our lives as so huge that we lose sight of the fact that God is bigger. But God's desire is that, with every new circumstance we face, we see not only the giant but also an opportunity to discover what he is capable of handling and just how big he really is.

The Power of Optimism

Life really is all about how we look at it. Chuck Swindoll, a well-known evangelical Christian pastor, author, educator, and radio preacher, once stated, "Life is 10 percent what happens to me, and 90 percent how I react to it." Life just happens, but attitude doesn't. A positive attitude that is pleasing to Christ and not poisoned by stress has to be developed over time, with commitment, dedication, perseverance, and self-discipline.

A Christ-like attitude—one that stays joyous and positive even in the midst of stressful circumstances and trusts that God is working even when it seems he is absent—is gradually built over a lifetime of submitting to God's desires over our own. Most people have at least one problem or worry that seems bigger than life. This problem may feel like a giant so large that you feel powerless to stand up and face it. If you feel like there is nothing you can do about the giants in your life, I want you to take a closer look at what those giants really are. I listed a few of the most common giants at the beginning of this chapter, all of which take an enormous toll on our hearts and drain our spirits. Maybe those are some of the giants you are facing today, and you may have some others to toss in the mix. But is the identifying label for the surface problem the actual problem? Or does the problem lie in the underlying perceptions about those problems, instead?

Could it be that fear, doubt, insecurity, and not believing that God really sees you are adding to how big the problem seems? Could it be that the way you perceive the problem, deal with the problem, and live with the problem are actually part of the problem? Could it be that your attitude is one of the biggest giants you face, more so than the situation you are facing?

Our attitude is a major contributing factor to how we handle our problems and how we manage our stress. I know that your problems are real. The circumstances may be scary and filling your heart with worry, and the outcome of the unknown may leave reason to be fearful. I am not downplaying the fact that true and overwhelming circumstances occur every day in our lives and that you may be hurting right now. I am simply suggesting that we take a closer look at the real root of the stress and see whether we can work through it so that you can become an overcomer.

Facing Your Giants

The first step to overcoming a giant is recognizing what the giant really is and confronting it face to face. The giant, whatever it is, is the only thing standing between you and victory.

In 1 Samuel 17, we learn about David and Goliath—a well-known story, with a well-known ending. But let's take a moment to dig a little deeper into what the real giant was for the army that stood helpless against the Philistines.

The Philistines and Israelites faced each other on opposite hills, with the valley between them. Then Goliath, a Philistine champion from Gath, came out of the Philistine ranks to face the forces of Israel. He was over nine feet tall! He wore a bronze helmet, and his bronze coat of mail weighed 125 pounds. He also wore bronze leg armor, and he carried a bronze javelin on his shoulder. The shaft of his spear was as heavy and thick as a weaver's beam, tipped with an iron spearhead that weighed 15 pounds. His armor bearer walked ahead of him carrying a shield. (vv. 3–7)

It was not necessarily this giant Philistine that made the Israelites feel hopeless about their victory. Instead, it was their attitude towards him. To the Israelites, it looked like there was no way to beat a creature of his stature and strength. Not only did they have this huge valley between themselves and the enemy but the enemy was also absolutely enormous. Can you imagine what he must have looked like based on the description we are given in the Bible?

If I had seen Goliath off in the distance, I probably would have reacted just like all of the Israelites who stayed safely in their tents on their side of the valley, cowering in fear at the sight of this monstrosity of a person.

Yet, even though Goliath was huge and threatening, the Israelites still longed for victory. Even though they thought victory was impossible, they still dreamed about it. There are issues in my life that seem as if they will never end, but I still want them to. The problem for the Israelites was they couldn't envision victory because their eyes were focused on the problem—Goliath.

The fear that Goliath created in them caused them to adopt an attitude of defeat. They were defeated long before the battle actually took place. The real giant that they needed to overcome was not the physical presence of Goliath but the mental presence of stress, worry, and fear in their hearts.

Goliath stood and shouted a taunt across to the Israelites. "Why are you all coming out to fight?" he called. "I am the Philistine champion, but you are only the servants of Saul. Choose one man to come down here and fight me! If he kills me, then we will be your slaves. But if I kill him, you will be our slaves! I defy the armies of Israel today! Send me a man who will fight me!" When Saul and the Israelites heard this, they were terrified and deeply shaken. (1 Sam. 17:8–11)

There was no joy in the hearts of the Israelites after hearing what Goliath had to say. They did not find his invitation amusing or inviting but so terrifying that it completely shook them up. Their defeat not only seemed imminent but they knew that someone would have to die and then they would all become slaves. Their fear not only stemmed from the potential threat of immediate death, for which no one wanted to volunteer, but also from imagining how horrible and tortuous daily life would be as servants of the Philistines. Their fears were paralyzing; their situation seemed hopeless. And, instead of calling out to God, even as their last resort, they hovered helplessly in the shadows of their fear.

Their attitude was not focused on God. They didn't think to call out to him for help. They didn't consider asking for a miracle, much less expect one. Instead, their eyes were focused on the giant, not on the God who had always been there for them. Just as we often forget, it never even crossed their minds to ask God for help in confronting their problem.

How often do you think we fall into that line of thinking? We find ourselves in a difficult position, faced with hardships, challenges, and hopelessness, but, instead of looking to the One who could make a difference, we look at how big the problem is and immediately begin spouting all the reasons why we cannot fight that battle.

We search within our own knowledge base for answers. We think we can do it by ourselves. We look to friends for advice. We seek out family members for support. We turn to co-workers for sympathy. We look to lawyers for justice. We look to counselors for therapy. We look to pastors for intercessory prayer. But we don't call out to God ourselves until we have exhausted every other possible avenue.

Victory does not merely come when the enemy is defeated but when we trust that God will have victory, no matter what our gut feelings are telling us. Real victory is when we learn to live with more joy and less stress, even when we can still see the giants looming off in the distance.

Goliath pranced in front of the Israelite army every morning and evening for forty days. It must have seemed to them that this problem would go on forever. But they were unaware that they would soon witness a miracle. David's father Jesse had eight sons, three of whom were in Saul's army. After a while, Jesse sent David to go and check on his brothers, take them some grain and bread, and report back to him about how they were getting along.

1 Samuel 17:20–23 says,

> So David left the sheep with another shepherd and set out early
> the next morning with the gifts, as Jesse had directed him. He
> arrived at the camp just as the Israelite army was leaving for the
> battlefield with shouts and battle cries. Soon the Israelite and
> Philistine forces stood facing each other, army against army.
> David left his things with the keeper of supplies and hurried out
> to the ranks to greet his brothers. As he was talking with them,
> Goliath, the Philistine champion from Gath, came out from the
> Philistine ranks. Then David heard him shout his usual taunt to
> the army of Israel.

One point that stands out to me about this passage is that, as soon as David heard what was happening, he "hurried out" to the battlefield to meet his brothers. The NIV translation says he "ran to the battle lines." David did not look at the battle line from afar, measure the distance that he would have to run versus his own quickness and agility, contemplate specific rock throwing moves, consider where he might be able to hide if things didn't work out, weigh all the positives against the negatives, or try to determine all the what-if scenarios so that he could be proactive and come up with solutions ahead of time. David just ran.

David did not hesitate in trusting that God was bigger than the giant, and, as a result, he stepped forward to confront Goliath with full confidence in God, not himself. We see him do this again after convincing his brothers that he was capable to fight the giant: "As Goliath moved closer to attack, David quickly ran out to meet him" (1 Sam. 17:48). Apparently, a lack of confidence was not something David struggled with, even though he was the baby in the family. But his confidence came from God—he knew that was all he needed to be strong.

So often our giants seem huge, especially when it comes to serious matters of life like finances, marriage, parenting, and health. The fear of these giants causes us to cower in the shadows, just like all those Israelites who saw their giant as a problem that could never be defeated. I have also found in my own experience that the longer I wait to confront a problem, the bigger that problem seems to get. But in any case, God is still bigger.

Are you facing a giant today? Is this giant causing you stress? Does it appear to be growing larger the longer you ignore it? Do you desire to be an overcomer of this particular giant and of your stress? Do you hunger for victory?

What is really stopping you from running to the battle line? The giant problem itself, or a giant lack of faith? Is your view of the giant making you so stressed that it is blocking your view of God? These are hard questions to ask ourselves, but uncovering the root of the problem is like putting a stone in our sling shot and knowing God will use it in powerful ways.

We usually want to see God at work before we will run to the battle line. But God wants us to make strides towards victory before he can do his best work—and victory begins when we are willing to run by faith, trusting that he will lead the way.

Running by Faith

The much-anticipated days of summer were finally here, and I was at my favorite place in the world—the beach. I hopped out of bed with an unusually eager attitude to do my morning exercise. As I stepped out of the door into the warm morning, seeing the sun rising in the sky and inhaling a deep breath of salty beach air, I immediately felt motivated to start my day. I headed for the soft sand. The subtle pounding of the waves hitting the shore sounded like music to my ears. I neared the edge of the surf and began jogging at a brisk pace.

After a short while, the morning sun became so exceptionally bright that it was hard to keep my eyes open at all. I reached for my sunglasses, which I thought were perched on my head, only to realize that in my haste to experience the beautiful Carolina surf I had left them behind.

Despite efforts to keep my eyes open, the brilliant sunshine straight in front of me across the vastness of the water was just too magnificent. I looked at the open area around me and decided it would be safe to go a short distance with my eyes closed completely. Knowing that miles of empty beach lay ahead of me and considering the fact that there were very few people at the beach this early in the morning, I closed my eyes tight and confidently ran forward. It was a strange feeling, one of vulnerability and slight concern, but, most importantly, one of trust. I had to trust that if I was going to run into anything or anyone, that someone would find it in their heart to warn me. Or at a minimum, not laugh when I plummeted face-first into the sand.

But, as I ran with my eyes closed, my heart opened wide and I began to pray. While talking with God, 2 Corinthians 5:7 came to mind: "We live by faith, not by sight" (NIV). Then a startling thought leapt into my mind: *I wonder if this is what God means when he tells us to walk by faith and not by sight?*

I allowed my mind to drift away from my surroundings and focus on this concept. In the case of my morning run, I already knew that there was nothing in my path to bump into. There were no people, dogs, umbrellas, or flying Frisbees out on the beach this early in the morning (especially since it was the middle of summer when most sane people were enjoying some extra sleep instead of sweating and panting in the sand). So I felt completely confident running with my eyes closed.

However, life does not always have a clutter-free pathway for us to run on, but rather is packed full of obstacles, big and small, and even a few giants. During my prayer time on this beautiful morning, I felt God nudging me to consider whether I would be willing to run with my eyes closed through the bumpy patches of life and solely rely on him for my confidence, even when I did not know what lay in front of me. Would I be willing to trust God's guidance, even when my own eyes could plainly see the obstacles or giants in my way?

I found myself asking God, *"Lord, please show me in which areas of my life I need to walk, and maybe run, by faith and not by sight. Where in my life do I not fully trust you?"*

For the next fifteen minutes, with each exhale of breath, God brought something or someone to mind that I needed to entrust to him—situations that I had been stressing over and people I had been worried about. A family member's terminal illness. A sister's battle with a chronic disease. A friend's slow-moving job search. A damaged relationship. A betrayal from someone I loved. A person I needed to forgive. Parenting. My marriage. Ministry. War. Our country. My future. My children's future.

It became crystal clear to me in that moment that I was rarely walking by faith regarding issues of great concern in my life. I recognized that even those times when I may think I am walking hand in hand with God, I may still find myself hiding behind a tree, deathly afraid of the giants that lie ahead in the valley, and assuming that victory can never be mine.

I sometimes feel more like the Israelites facing Goliath than I would like to admit. I, too, am guilty of trying to figure out my own problems and carry my own burdens. I fret and worry. I imagine the worst case scenario. I try to determine what I can do to remedy the problem. I waste time wishing things were different when I should be walking with my eyes closed in faith, giving God the opportunity to do his work.

Worrying cannot change a thing, but faith can change everything. We can put our faith in God, believing with full confidence that he will take care of the obstacles, guide us around the problems, and carry us through to the end.

To take this a step further, let's remember that we are not commanded to merely walk by faith, but to *live* by faith each and every day. This holy instruction challenges me. You see, I don't want to simply walk by faith; I want to run by faith. I want to run towards the victory with full confidence that God has everything under control, even when I have no clue how he will come through. I just want to have enough faith to trust that he will.

I want to have the type of faith in Christ that will allow me to close my physical eyes and see through the eyes of my heart, instead—to believe that God can fight my giants and that the victory has already been won. And that is an attitude worth fighting for.

An Attitude like His

Jesus had every reason to have a bad attitude. In the thirty-three years that Jesus walked the earth, he experienced immense hardships, heartaches, and stress. He experienced every emotion imaginable through celebrations, threats, joy, intense grief, overwhelming sorrow, looming disappointments, life interruptions, ridiculous demands, daily pressures, rejection, temptation, hurt, embarrassment, betrayal, and loneliness. So, when we go through really hard times, facing those huge giants that seem to be sucking the life right out of our hearts, we can find solace in knowing that Jesus understands how we feel.

Maybe today you are experiencing one or many of those emotions above. Maybe you feel like nobody understands what you are going through and no one can relate to what you are feeling. But friend, Jesus understands how you feel, even if it seems that no one else does.

In his book *In The Eye Of The Storm* Max Lucado writes,

When Matthew writes that Jesus had compassion on the people, he is not saying that Jesus felt casual pity for them. No, the term is far more graphic. Matthew is saying that Jesus felt their hurt in his gut:

- He felt the limp of the crippled.
- He felt the hurt of the diseased.
- He felt the loneliness of the leper.
- He felt the embarrassment of the sinful.

And once He felt their hurts, He couldn't help but heal their hurts. He was moved in the stomach by their needs. He was so touched by their needs that He forgot His own needs. He was so moved by the people's hurts that He put His hurts on the back burner.[21]

This brief paragraph from the book beautifully portrays the immense compassion Jesus has for us, as well as his immense understanding of our feelings and our stress.

He understands how we feel not only because he walked the earth as God in human flesh but also because his love for us causes him to actually feel our hurts. He doesn't merely catch our every tear and desire to comfort us; he actually shares our pain, physically and emotionally. But regardless of the disappointments and pain that Jesus suffered in his body on our behalf, what we can hopefully take away from this understanding is the incredible realization that, despite all of his sufferings, Jesus never wavered in his attitude.

Jesus never got mad in sin and refused to forgive someone. Jesus never betrayed someone because she had betrayed him. Jesus never turned away from someone in need. Jesus never gossiped about anyone behind his back. Jesus never lacked compassion. Jesus was never selfish. Jesus was never prideful. Jesus was never rebellious or vengeful. Jesus was never unrighteous in his thoughts or actions. Jesus never looked for the bad in anything or anyone. His attitude was not founded on the shifting sand of his earthly circumstances, his earthly surroundings, or his human feelings. It was grounded on the Rock of Salvation, the Father who was bigger than anything he could encounter.

Despite how he was treated, the challenges he faced, the persecution he endured, and the pain he suffered, Jesus' attitude remained one of love, compassion, and optimism. He was able to look past the present to see the future benefits. He knew the truth found in Romans 8:28 that everything serves a higher purpose to glorify God for those who are loved and called by him. Oh, to have an attitude like his.

A few years ago I read a story about some women shopping in a bookstore. One lady was already browsing the shelves when two other women walked in. One was absolutely stunning—you couldn't help but stare at her. Her features, mannerisms, and elegant clothing looked like they were swiped off the cover of a glamour magazine. Next to this beautiful woman was her friend, who was in a wheelchair. This young woman was somewhat plain looking, slightly overweight, wearing no makeup, and possessed no real sense of style or fashion.

They were an odd pair to be out together, but the lady didn't think about it anymore and went back to her browsing. A few minutes later, she could hear the pair talking in the next aisle. One was gently coaxing the other: "It's just your attitude. You can do anything you set your mind to. Life is wonderful; it's all about how we choose to see things. You have so many things to be thankful for. Just try to focus on your blessings."

The bystander didn't mean to eavesdrop, but it was easy to get transfixed on the conversation. The uplifting words and the pleasant voice were so powerful that she almost believed them herself.

After all, she was listening to the words of an obviously beautiful and successful woman. But that thought snapped the lady back to reality, and she felt a twinge of anger. She began to think, *Well, it's easy for her to talk about having a positive attitude when she has everything. Beauty. Money. A perfect body. Health. Gorgeous clothes. Success.* Her attitude after eavesdropping quickly turned from optimism to cynicism.

But when the lady rounded the corner, she stopped dead in her tracks. She saw the two women who had been talking and realized that the encouraging voice, the powerful, positive message overflowing with optimism had come from the lips of the woman in the wheelchair.

Oh, to have an outlook on life like that precious woman in the wheelchair. An attitude of hope and a perspective of love, despite having many reasons to have a negative outlook. An innate ability to look at the good things in life, instead of focusing on the negative aspects. A desire to encourage others to be positive, even when our own circumstances may be negative. An attitude that allows us to be happy for the blessings of others, even when we are still waiting. I can only imagine how happy life would be if we could stay so grounded in our faith that we would never waver in our positive attitudes.

We obviously cannot achieve this with absolute perfection, but we have been promised the grace to try—grace to learn from our mistakes, to face the battles when they come, to fail and be forgiven, and to always receive that second chance, time and time again.

We are provided with grace sufficient to defeat our giants one by one, if only we trust God for the victory. Grace to recognize that even when we are battling a raging monster of the heart, God is still the answer.

But I Feel Forgotten

God loves us too much to make life easy. In fact, there may even be times when God keeps us in a battle in order to take us to a place where we can experience his presence and get some hands-on practice at building an attitude like Jesus'.

You may be experiencing a season of life where God seems to be a million miles away. A season where you are wondering why he is allowing a certain hardship in your life, especially if you have already been devoted to loving him, serving him, and trusting his ways.

There was a time not too long ago when, faced with a certain problem, I had some of those types of thoughts. As my emotions started playing tricks on my mind, I allowed my anxieties and fears to get the better of me, and I began to feel further and further from God—completely helpless, rejected, and utterly alone.

In retrospect, I can see how God used those difficult times to help me learn that my responses to situations could teach me a lot about real faith, and that, in times of crisis, those responses could either make me or break me. Those situations could make me stronger if I continued to trust God in all his ways, even when I didn't like or understand them. Or they could break me if I turned away from God in anger and frustration, giving the devil a foothold in my heart.

We all experience those feelings of rejection and loneliness at one time or another, whether as a little girl who desperately wishes her daddy would love her, an employee who longs for the acceptance of her boss, a mom whose heart aches for a close relationship with her teen, or a woman who would give anything to have her husband show her some affection.

There are many types of rejections, but feeling forgotten by a Sovereign God can definitely hurt the worst.

In Psalm 43, we read about how the psalmist felt rejected and forgotten by God. He writes, "Declare me innocent, O God! Defend me against these ungodly people. Rescue me from these unjust liars. For you are God, my only safe haven. Why have you tossed me aside? Why must I wander around in grief, oppressed by my enemies?" (Ps. 43: 1–2). The NIV Bible actually uses the word rejection when it says in verse 2, "You are God my stronghold. Why have you rejected me?"

He felt rejected by God. Forgotten. Alone. Weak. Confused. Frustrated. He was at such a low point, he even began questioning God, asking why he was not acting on his behalf and why he was allowing him to suffer. Can you relate? I certainly can. Shall I say, "Been there, done that . . . more than once"?

But then, in verses three and four, it seems that the psalmist had some kind of personal revelation, suddenly remembering that God truly was his only help: "Send out your light and your truth; let them guide me. Let them lead me to your holy mountain, to the place where you live. There I will go to the altar of God, to God—the source of all my joy. I will praise you with my harp, O God, my God!"

The psalmist recognized his own weakness and his need for God. He pleaded for God's guidance and intervention in his life and then promised his faithfulness in return. In the midst of his suffering, he chose to willfully and wholeheartedly praise God. He walked in faith, not by sight.

In verse 5 we see the psalmist change his attitude completely: "Why am I discouraged? Why is my heart so sad? I will put my hope in God! I will praise him again—my Savior and my God!" I am only guessing here, but it appears that he recognized that his sour attitude was not helping the situation. He realized that, despite his circumstances, a bad attitude was only making things worse. It's almost like he was telling himself to "snap out of it!" So he called out for the strength to change, from the inside out.

The psalmist apparently decided to stop listening to that inner voice that had been taunting his self-worth, condemning his self-esteem, and pulling him into a pit of despair and discouragement. He chose to change his attitude, to cry out to God for help, and seek guidance, strength, and the will to persevere.

At times we may find ourselves wrestling with which voice to listen to, but this passage in Psalm 43 reassures us that we too can overcome stress during the battle if we seek out God's face in the midst of it. We can have troubles and still be in God's favor, as we allow him to be our strength.

During stressful situations, or just days when we feel overwhelmed and pulled in every direction, our thoughts can quickly be lured into wondering, *Where is God in all of this?* We wrestle with the thought of being rejected by God. In the midst of our heartaches, it is easy to listen to the voice of the enemy who wants us to believe that God has left us to face life alone. It is easy to allow our circumstances to divide our hearts, resulting in an inner emotional struggle over whom to believe, what to believe, and whom to turn to. Yet we are reminded in Hebrews 13:5 that God made a promise, "Never will I leave you; never will I forsake you" (NIV). If we believe God's Word is infallible and true, then we must also believe this promise without a shadow of a doubt. Even when we feel abandoned, it's so important that we not allow our feelings to diminish the value of our faith. When our faith is grounded in the Word of God and we are receiving those daily portions from him, we are so much better equipped to tackle these questions when they arise and to keep our minds on track with the truth.

As we focus on our relationship with Christ on a daily basis, on carefree days and crazy days, we will be spiritually nourished to fight the battle of the mind, heart, and soul if and when a battle does begin. We will be prepared to preach to ourselves, just like the psalmist did and focus on remembering what we believe and whom we believe in.

Giants are big. Giants are ugly. Giants are scary. But in God's eyes, all giants are beatable. Because God is bigger.

Reflection Questions

1. What giants have you been facing that seem too big for God? List them here.

2. How can you begin to trust God to help you face these giants through his strength?

3. Does your stress come from the problems you face or from the way you react to those problems?

4. Are there any changes you can make in your behavior to begin confronting these issues in more productive ways? List some here.

5 . Is it possible that you have a bad attitude, which might be contributing to your stress? Explain or reflect on some of the situations where this has happened. This is a difficult question to answer, but be honest with yourself and with God. Meaningful change cannot occur if we are hesitant to confess our own shortcomings and our need for God's help.

6. What areas of your attitude might you need to work on? Look up some Bible verses about attitude, and consider memorizing them to refer to in daily prayer. List some of the verses you selected here:

7. Do you truly believe that God is sovereign and capable of handling your problems? Write a brief prayer to God professing your trust in him.

Stress Busting Scriptures

Therefore do not worry about tomorrow, for tomorrow will worry about itself. Each day has enough trouble of its own.

Matthew 6:34 NIV

I sought the LORD, and he answered me; he delivered me from all my fears.

Psalm 34:4 NIV

The LORD will guide you always; he will satisfy your needs in a sun-scorched land and will strengthen your frame. You will be like a well-watered garden, like a spring whose waters never fail.

Isaiah 58:11 NIV

Get rid of all bitterness, rage, anger, harsh words, and slander, as well as all types of evil behavior. Instead, be kind to each other, tenderhearted, forgiving one another, just as God through Christ has forgiven you.

Ephesians 4:31–32

And now, dear brothers and sisters, one final thing. Fix your thoughts on what is true, and honorable, and right, and pure, and lovely, and admirable. Think about things that are excellent and worthy of praise.

Philippians 4:8

Chapter Eight

Addicted to Adrenaline

Einstein famously said that the definition of insanity is doing the same thing over and over and expecting different results. Sometimes, however, even when we know we are insanely worried, busy, and stressed—speeding through life without ever stopping to enjoy it while wishing that something would change—it is our addiction to adrenaline that compels us to continue the insane behavior.

The world today has become so fast paced that any deviance from busyness is actually viewed as sinful. When people consider the stereotypes of those who are addicted to adrenaline, successful businessmen and businesswomen come to mind. Executives from all industries have been pulled into the dangerous, chaotic world of never-ending corporate busyness, fueled by a constant rush of dangerous adrenaline.

These people are usually seen typing on their smartphones at every waking moment. They run from task to task, thriving on their hurried pace, eating on the go, always toting their laptop or iPad, and feeling as if any deceleration of the speed of their lives would be seen as a negative personal attribute.

They are under the impression that they must keep their engine at full throttle at all times. They never cease to multitask. Their identity is dependent on how much they can get done and how quickly they can do it. Some even carry their stress like a badge of honor. When other people acknowledge their busyness or their high level of productivity, it recharges their overworked battery and propels them forward. When they wonder in private how their life got so chaotic, however, they wish things were different. But, despite the harm it may cause them, they continue in their cycle of addiction.

Just as a race car is fueled by gasoline, their bodies are fueled by the natural hormone our bodies produce when we are under stress—epinephrine (a.k.a. adrenaline). Epinephrine is released when our bodies are faced with either excitement or stress. Elizabeth Scott describes the responses of this release:

> Epinephrine is a naturally occurring hormone. During the fight-or-flight response, the adrenal gland releases epinephrine into the blood stream, along with other hormones like cortisol, signaling the heart to pump harder, increasing blood pressure, opening airways in the lungs, narrowing blood vessels in the skin and intestine to increase blood flow to major muscle groups, and performing other functions to enable the body to fight or run when encountering a perceived threat.[22]

Epinephrine can be good when someone is faced with a life-threatening crisis, such as needing superhuman strength to lift a wrecked car off of a person trapped underneath. But when this hormone constantly secretes into our bodies because of unrelenting stress, it can be extremely harmful to our health.

But business people are not the only ones who thrive on or get addicted to adrenaline. In some cases, this addiction to busyness is present in people who do not work in an office at all, such as stay-at-home moms or dads. They spend every waking moment changing diapers, cleaning the house, fixing meals, buying groceries, sewing on buttons, administering medicine, driving to play dates, coaching cheerleading squads or sports teams, helping with community service projects, caring for sick family members, serving on church committees, mowing the lawn, planting the flowers, and paying bills.

What about the hardworking, blue collar class, such as third-shift employees who spend all night working and then all day doing the things mentioned above? People from every job category can become addicted to the thrill of adrenaline.

Finally, let's not forget all of those thrill seekers who willingly step into dangerous situations in pursuit of an adrenaline rush, thriving on the emotional high they get from risking their lives in pursuit of adventure. Extreme sports such as parachute jumping, hang gliding, sky diving, mountain climbing, skiing, and bungee jumping bring high risk. Just in the past year, several backcountry skiers who were skiing in avalanche-prone areas met unfortunate ends. Even though there is a high level of inherent danger in many extreme sports, people still participate in them because of their addictions to adrenaline. The chance that I would do any of these activities is less than slim to none. My idea of taking a real risk is getting on an airplane and sitting in the exit row.

But even cautious people like myself can put their lives in jeopardy by living lives of chronic stress. Whether we are risk takers or not, the gravitational pull into a life of busyness is almost impossible to avoid, and we can easily become addicted to adrenaline before we even realize what is happening.

An addiction to adrenaline is often difficult to diagnose because it pushes us beyond what is healthy under the guise of normal life. People who are addicted will find that they make sure that they are doing something . . . all the time. There is never room for down time because that would mean they are not needed or they may feel unproductive. The rush they receive from busyness keeps them going from day to day; they relish in the compliments and pats on the back received from others. Their minds are fueled by the praise, and they can't even fathom taking a day of rest.

On the flip side of this discussion, some people thrive on an insane addiction to adrenaline simply as an attempt to keep their focus on anything that distracts them from the pain and heartbreak of their past or the stressful adversities in their present. They keep busy to prevent themselves from thinking about the burdens on their heart or the problems in their life. They keep busy in order to avoid dealing with relationships. But, eventually, the outcome is the same and their adrenaline gives them a rush that they can no longer live without.

No matter what the root cause of adrenaline addiction may be, adrenaline junkies are always overwhelmed, pulled in every direction (often by choice), and stressed to the max. They thrive on the need to feel necessary and productive and possess an insatiable sense of urgency and need for accomplishment. If anything comes up that derails their well-laid-out plans, sheer panic could potentially set in.

I know all of this to be true because I once was an adrenaline junkie. Hello. My name is Tracie, and I am a recovering adrenaline junkie. What about you?

Is There Hope for Me?

Being an adrenaline junkie is a dangerous affliction, but we do have hope for recovery in Jesus. Yet the biggest problem faced by adrenaline junkies is admitting they actually are addicted.

Addiction to adrenaline causes a domino effect of consequences, with the majority of the damage happening to the junkie him- or herself. (Case in point: the overwhelming health issues I experienced before resigning from my corporate position and the weakened state of my spiritual heart before I finally sought recovery.) The problem goes back to the "new normal" I talked about earlier. If your new normal is a life consumed with stress and achievement and busyness, you may not even realize that you are thriving on an adrenaline rush every day. You may not even know that you are an adrenaline junkie. Maybe you don't mean to be an adrenaline junkie, but life has created a monster in you. Or maybe you are just in denial.

Unlike a drug addict who deliberately ingests the drugs, adrenaline junkies don't even know they are poisoning themselves, making it a more dangerous drug than one would think. It is a drug that can harm our bodies, our marriages, our families, our friendships, and our overall lives. Eventually, we will reach the breaking point. A point of exhaustion and burnout. A point where we cease to enjoy daily living but feel helpless to make a change. A point where we feel trapped by our lifestyle but have no idea how to escape.

And there are even more serious consequences (many of which I have already mentioned). In October 2007, a study published in the *Journal of the American Medical Association* (*JAMA*) showed significant links between stress and heart attacks and heart disease.

> The *JAMA* study, led by researchers at the Université Laval in Quebec, finds that first-time heart attack patients who returned to chronically stressful jobs were twice as likely to have a second attack as patients whose occupations were relatively stress-free. The study tracked 972 first-time heart attack survivors, aged 35–59, all of whom went back to work within 18 months of their heart attack for at least 10 hours a week. In periodic follow-up interviews between 1996 and 2005, those patients who reported chronic job strain—defined as a job that was high in psychological demands but low in feelings of control—were not only at higher risk for a second heart attack, but also had a markedly higher risk of death than their less-stressed peers.[23]

Dr. Archibald Hart, in his book titled *Adrenaline and Stress*, provides an in-depth look at the links between an addiction to adrenaline and heart disease. Lastly, in the *Yoga Journal*, Dr. Dharma Singh Khalsa says the stress response of "near-constant cortisol release (from the adrenal gland) can damage the memory center of the brain [causing us to] lose our ability to concentrate, and recall."[24] He also relates that the brain becomes less capable at managing the chemical release with age.

Have you ever noticed that when you are trying to juggle multiple projects at once, sick with worry about a specific problem, or fretting over all the things on your to-do list you have a hard time focusing? No matter how proficient we may think we are at multitasking, our brains may have trouble keeping up with our self-imposed obligation to do it all, and all of it at the same time. When we are tired or stressed or overwhelmed, we may find that focusing on the task at hand, concentrating with full clarity, and maintaining accuracy become more difficult. Thinking may become clouded, and memory may become scattered simply because your brain is on overload.

Maybe you have gone through a time when you found yourself having a hard time focusing or concentrating because of the never ceasing demands on your time or the mountain of stressors that were piling up before you. If so, you will be interested in another consequence of stress that Dr. Khalsa mentions. Dr. Khalas's studies are primarily associated with treating Alzheimer's disease. Scary? I agree.

Living in a constant state of stress, with adrenaline dangerously coursing through our veins, like a cancer cell just waiting for a place to land, will eventually lead to serious consequences, including heart attacks, Alzheimer's, and possibly death. So, you see, even if our physical health somehow manages to escape serious problems (although highly unlikely), the mental and emotional damage that is inflicted can be fatal as well.

Is it possible that you are an adrenaline junkie? Is it possible you are putting yourself at risk by ignoring the problem of stress in your life?

If you have never thought of stress as a problem for you and you think you can handle the busyness of life without skipping a beat, are you beginning to second-guess yourself after reading this information? My prayer is that your answer is a confident "yes." But if you are still unsure or afraid to say no with full assurance, then take a look at these types of adrenaline junkies and see if you identify with one of them.

According to the 2005 *Leadership Review*, published by the Kravis Leadership Institute at Claremont McKenna College in Claremont, California, there are four types of adrenaline junkies. Although some of this content is directed towards workplace issues, overall it is a fantastic way to categorize what type of stress addiction each of us may be facing:

1. The Accomplisher—this is the classic type of adrenaline addict, the one who has an almost innate need to stay busy and cross things off a list in order to feel productive. They like to be able to measure daily progress in terms of what they have completed, even at the expense of the bigger, longer-term view. Accomplishers are most susceptible to developing an adrenaline addiction because they are prone to take on more and more work.

2. The Personal Deflector—this is the type that uses their addiction to keep from assessing themselves and reflecting on their situation. They often have problems in their personal lives—or no personal life at all—and the last thing they want to do is face up to that. So they convince themselves that they have no time for their personal lives; which, sadly, only exacerbates the problem and prolongs the pain of dealing with it.

3. The Organizational Deflector—this type is like the previous one, except that the issue being avoided is trouble within the organization (for the sake of our discussion, one could ponder if their issue is avoiding trouble within their home or personal life). Often a CEO or senior executive of a struggling company convinces him- or herself, as well as others, that he or she is too busy to stop and take an honest look at the company's situation (in the same way, one might be too busy to take an honest look at their personal problems). As the company spirals (or our lives spiral), the adrenaline addict only works harder, trying to be convinced that the problem can be solved by working more hours at breakneck speed. The organizational deflector will do anything to avoid confronting the real problems, which are often more complex and require real change.

4. The Dramatist—some adrenaline addicts get a degree of satisfaction from their addiction because it gives them an opportunity to draw attention to themselves and their plight. They complain about and describe their overwhelming situation, seemingly seeking admiration or pity from those upon whom they unload their problems.[25]

Do you see yourself in one of these descriptions? I would venture to say that the majority of people reading this book can identify with at least one category. Stress is rampant in our society, so to think that any person is immune to it, or can handle it with ease, is painfully unrealistic.

But there is hope for us adrenaline junkies. The sooner we recognize that we have been inadvertently pulled into a lifestyle of incredible busyness, chaos, and overcommitment, the sooner we can begin to reach for healing. We can stare our reality in the face and work towards purposely trying to prevent all of these physical, mental, and spiritual problems from occurring.

Seeking awareness is the first step. Seeking Jesus is the second.

A Step towards Healing

I once heard an old cliché that said, if the devil can't hinder our relationship with God by making us immoral, he'll simply make us busy. If we take a good hard look around, there are a lot of godly people who are too busy for Jesus. Let's face it, if we are too busy to spend time with God, then we are absolutely way too busy! Just as spending too little time with our family and loved ones results in damaged relationships, spending too little time with Jesus can damage our relationship with him.

The Bible tells us that one day we will all stand in front of God, accountable for our actions, which includes being held accountable for how we spent our time and what kept us busy all of our lives. "For we must all stand before Christ to be judged. We will each receive whatever we deserve for the good or evil we have done in this earthly body" (2 Cor. 5:10).

Knowing that one day we will have to account for our lives should compel us to ask ourselves the hard questions: What is keeping me most busy? Where do I devote the majority of my time? What calls for my attention most often? What am I neglecting? What should I let go of? Is my time well spent? Will I be proud to talk with God about how I spent most of my time on earth?

In many cases, our answers to these first questions may be primarily from the categories of work or family. These are important aspects of life that are necessary to spend our time on, and God calls us to be diligent and devoted to both. However, when we allow even the good things of life to become deterrents to our spiritual lives and cause us chronic stress, then changes are necessary.

John 9:4 says, "We must quickly carry out the tasks assigned us by the one who sent us. The night is coming, and then no one can work." Here we see Jesus telling his disciples that they were to be busy with God's business. Not just busy with impressive acts of service but busy using their time wisely and in big and small ways in their everyday lives that would glorify God. Psalm 39:5–7 says, "You have made my life no longer than the width of my hand. My entire lifetime is just a moment to you; at best, each of us is but a breath. We are merely moving shadows, and all our busy rushing ends in nothing. We heap up wealth, not knowing who will spend it. And so, Lord, where do I put my hope? My only hope is in you."

When David wrote the psalm above, he was acknowledging that life was short and that we should therefore focus our time on the types of busyness, and business, that really matter. He realized that going through life apart from God was meaningless and that his only hope for real happiness, peace, and joy was in Christ.

How God's heart longs for us to embrace the desire to be rescued by his hope, just like David did.

The Rescuer

One sunny spring day fourteen years ago, my family and I had driven over to my mother's house for a quick visit. While we were there, she mentioned that there was a family heirloom she wanted to give to me, but it was stored away in the attic. I instructed my four-year-old daughter, Morgan, to stay downstairs with her daddy while I went with my mother to the attic. I proceeded up to the second floor of the house holding my eighteen-month-old daughter, Kaitlyn.

As I was searching for the box in the attic, Kaitlyn was toddling around the cramped room, curiously checking out the strange surroundings, while looking extremely cute and inquisitive, as little girls do. As I began searching in one particular area of the attic, Kaitlyn pattered across the bare wooden floor in her new, white walking shoes, wandering just a few feet away. Just as I looked up to call her back towards me, she vanished. In a split second, she was gone.

As it turned out, there was a hole in the attic floor that my mother was not even aware existed. A hole just big enough for a baby to fall straight through with ease.

For the first time in my entire life, I involuntarily screamed in sheer horror. I could not stop screaming. My heart stopped as fear filled every bone in my body. It was as if time stood still. My legs felt as heavy as lead as I tried to frantically rush to the exact spot where she had been standing just one second earlier. It was then that I saw the gaping hole for the very first time. As I glared down the spot where my baby once stood, my eyes caught a glimpse of her as she plummeted downward, just before she impacted with the ground. As my eyes were locked on her fall in horror, my mind could not grasp the reality that my child was potentially plunging to her death on the hard concrete garage floor twenty feet below.

But when her fall came to an abrupt halt, I witnessed a miracle. A rescue, above all rescues that I had ever or would ever be blessed to see. I watched as her tiny little body collided with the ground and bounced off of the hard concrete floor . . . like a soft rubber ball. It was as if she had landed on a fluffy pillow of cotton, or even a tiny trampoline, and just gingerly bounced off. My mind raced with confusion, but the numbing fear that had overtaken my body left me no mental capacities to try to process what I thought I had seen.

With all of this happening in less than a few seconds, I continued to scream and tears began to hinder my vision. As soon as I saw her impact, I flew down the stairwell at the speed of lighting, panicked and unable to breathe, taking three and four steps at a time, my mother right at my heels.

I ran through the house, flung open the garage door, and saw my precious baby lying there motionless on the floor. I gently scooped her up in my arms. I have never heard a sound so precious as the sound of her cries in that moment. But sheer terror set in as I imagined the internal damage that had surely been incurred by her fall. I wondered if her skull or any other tiny bones were cracked or shattered, although I could not see any damage with the naked eye.

My poor husband, bless his heart, was absolutely terror stricken, having no idea what the sudden commotion was about. When he finally found me sobbing hysterically in the garage, holding our wailing little girl, the blood drained from his face as the reality of what had occurred sunk into his brain. We immediately dashed to the car and rushed to the emergency room as thoughts of the worst filled our hearts and minds.

Strangely, by the time we arrived at the hospital twenty minutes later, Kaitlyn's tears had dried and she was acting like her normal, cute little self. My husband and I exchanged worried glances, as we sat in the ER waiting room for what seemed like an eternity. With each breath I took, my worry increased. *Why wasn't she crying? Was she in shock? Did she have a concussion? Did she have brain damage? Or worse? Oh God, please see us. See our little girl.*

When we finally saw the doctor and explained what had happened, a perplexing look washed across his face. Instead of ordering MRIs and X-rays, he was unsuccessfully trying to keep Kaitlyn from grabbing the stethoscope around his neck. As he gently tried to examine her little body, she giggled with delight.

He could find no injuries, other than a small egg-shaped bump on one side of her forehead. There was no external or internal bleeding, and she did not have a scratch, bruise, concussion, or broken bone in her little fragile body. The doctor told us that had I not told him I witnessed the fall, he would seriously doubt whether it actually happened.

Kaitlyn was completely unharmed, but I was transformed. Do you think it was luck that my baby was unharmed after such a horrific incident? Absolutely not. We walked out of the ER with a renewed faith and a life-giving gratitude for her Rescuer. Our Rescuer.

I believe with my whole heart that God rescued my baby from a fall that should have killed her. My only explanation for what I saw is that an angel was sent to her rescue in that very moment and caught my precious child in the safety of her soft, white as snow, beautiful wings. Or maybe God himself stepped in and leaned down from his throne in his most perfect and precise timing, catching Kaitlyn securely in the palm of his loving, mighty hands.

Either way, Psalm 91:4 took on a whole new meaning for me that day. "He will cover you with his feathers. He will shelter you with his wings. His faithful promises are your armor and protection." My child found protection, safety, and life in the wings of God. He faithfully rescued and protected one of his children, who just happened to also be one of mine. But this rescue was not only for my baby; it was for me. I was speechless at the favor God had bestowed upon my child, and I vowed to never doubt the vastness of God's love for me again. The miracle that happened in this situation is beyond our human capacity to grasp, but there is simply no other explanation than God's hand at work.

Sweet friend, do you need to be rescued today? Do you feel like your life is spiraling out of control, consumed with stress, worry, and busyness? Do you feel like you are plummeting downward, wondering how hard your impact will be? Do you need someone to put your hope in because the situations in your life seem hopeless and change seems impossible? Have you been living off the rush of adrenaline, addicted to its power over your heart and your life?

Remember this . . . God is not only capable of rescuing us from physical harm but also from emotional and mental harm, as well. He longs to be our rescuer, even when we are blinded to the fact that we need to be rescued.

In 2 Samuel 22, David sings a song of praise to the Lord for delivering him from his enemies. I find it interesting, however, that before the Lord acted, David had to ask to be rescued: "But in my distress I cried out to the LORD; yes, I cried to my God for help. He heard me from his sanctuary; my cry reached his ears" (v. 7). Then we see that David thanks God for his rescue in verse 33: "It is God who arms me with strength and makes my way perfect" (NIV).

David faced more adversity than we would want to shake a stick at, but he remained strong in his faith by relying on a holy strength that he could not muster on his own. He didn't choose a slingshot as his weapon, he chose God.

Sometimes we may feel like we are running a close second to David in the race for the worst adversity. But, just as it was for David, strength and rescue is available for each one of us. All we have to do is ask and believe that God will work on our behalf and give us what we need to overcome and rise above the adversities and stress that we are facing. When we seek his deliverance, like David did, God first gives us the strength to persevere, then he provides the rescue.

If you are willing to admit that stress has become a problem in your life and that just maybe you are even an addict, then take a moment right now and ask God to rescue you. Believe with your whole heart that he will do just that. Envision his mighty hand stretching down from the heavens, ready to catch you and deliver you from the toxin of stress.

In God's Strength

If you just paused and prayed, asking God to rescue your heart from whatever has been holding your joy and freedom captive, then I rejoice with you! Today is the first day of the rest of your life in his strength. If you have admitted to yourself that you just might be an adrenaline junkie— living a life overloaded with stress and busyness, filled with an overflow of emotions that are increasingly taking a toll on your mind, body, and soul—then today could be the first day of your "new normal."

Change is often hard, awkward, and uncomfortable. When it comes to saving your life, however, change can become mandatory. But thanks to Jesus, we do not have to strive for change in our own strength (or lack of strength).

Four years ago, my stepmother was diagnosed with cancer. She went through all of the necessary treatments, and we were thrilled beyond belief when her doctor announced the good news of her remission. Unfortunately, a year later the cancer returned. Although she went through the standard rounds of chemotherapy and radiation treatments again, her body was not responding and the cancer continued to spread. After a long and fiercely fought battle, her tenure on earth was drawing to a close. My husband and I arranged to make the four-hour trip with our children to go and visit her, knowing that it might possibly be for the last time.

I walked into her hospital room and found her lying in the bed looking very weak and frail, helpless to beat the disease that had waged war on her body. I fought back the tears as I struggled with my own feelings of helplessness. My deepest sorrow came bubbling up to the surface as I tried with all my might to fight back the tears. I found myself wanting to do something for her, anything . . . but there was nothing I could do except wish to the depths of my heart that I could infuse her with the strength she needed to carry on. But I felt weak and had no strength to give, and, even if I did, my strength held no power.

Later that day, after returning home with a heavy heart, I looked to God's Word for comfort. I came across two verses that seeped deep into the cracks in my heart that so needed to be filled with God: "Therefore, be careful to obey every command I am giving you today, so you may have strength to go in and take over the land you are about to enter. If you obey, you will enjoy a long life in the land the LORD swore to give your ancestors and to you, their descendants—a land flowing with milk and honey!" (Deut. 11:8–9).

At first glance this verse may not seem even remotely relevant to what I was going through, but God had a special message in mind for me. In this passage the Lord is telling the Israelites about their soon-to-be entrance into the Promised Land. He had been reminding them of all the miracles and amazing things that had happened during their journey. He knew, based on their history of sinful actions and attitudes, that they were easily tempted by idols, which had caused them to lose their focus on God and be devoid of strength.

In these verses, we find the Lord warning the Israelites about losing sight of their priorities, reminding them that the only place they will find strength is in him. The Lord also wanted them to understand that their strength could not come from merely carrying out rituals or sacrifices in his honor—strength would only come from full obedience. In fact, in Deuteronomy 11:18 the Lord says, "So commit yourselves wholeheartedly to these words of mine. Tie them to your hands and wear them on your forehead as reminders."

Their strength could only come from wholehearted obedience to all of the Lord's commands. They were to even wear his words on their hands and foreheads so that they would never forget them. And even today— in our society of rampant busyness, unrelenting stress, and adrenaline addictions—God wants us to do the same. His desire is that we come to understand the importance of walking with him every day, because that is where we gain our strength. If you are trying to be strong in adversity and in good times based solely on your own strength, skills, or knowledge, then stress is the only possible outcome. You do not have the power within to maintain the strength needed to persevere, and you will soon find that real rest and relaxation seem unattainable.

God instructs us to obey in the big things, of course, but also in our small, seemingly insignificant daily thoughts and actions. This obedience infuses us with a spiritual strength that equips us to handle those tough situations that are far beyond our human level of strength to handle, regardless of whether we are in the hospital bed or standing beside it.

This daily obedience is where we find the infusion of emotional strength that allows us to walk in his peace when we face doubts and fears. Strength to walk in his joy when we cannot find any reason to be joyful. Strength to stand firm in our faith when things seem hopeless. And strength to be strong when the painful things of life are taking their toll on our hearts.

Most importantly, our desire to walk with God on a daily basis gives us the strength to not only acknowledge that changes need to be made but to believe that he will provide the strength and the wisdom to decipher which changes we need.

Each day when we get out of bed, we have a choice to make about where our strength will come from to face the day ahead. Will we rely on ourselves or will we rely on God? Will we try to rely on our human strength to persevere, or will we seek the strength that God provides to our spirits, enabling us to get through even the most painful of days? Will we continue to assume that if we try hard enough we will have the power to change or make changes happen, or will we realize that God, and God alone, possesses the power to do so?

If your life is stressful, chaotic, busy, and overloaded, then I imagine your heart is tired and your body is weak. Maybe you feel like you are dangling over a pit, dangerously close to the end of your rope. Maybe you feel as I did, standing by my stepmother's hospital bed, aching for the power to make things better, while feeling weighed down by the heavy burden of my helplessness.

Maybe you want to be strong, but you have no strength left to lift life's weights from your heart. If so, maybe now you realize that stress has taken its toll and you are finally ready to change and be changed.

Take comfort in reading Matthew 11:28–29: "Then Jesus said, 'Come to me, all of you who are weary and carry heavy burdens, and I will give you rest. Take my yoke upon you. Let me teach you, because I am humble and gentle at heart, and you will find rest for your souls.'"

Do you see the sweet promise? Not only for rest but for peace in your heart? Are you ready to spend some time in God's presence, soaking in these Scriptures and letting him teach you how to make the promises in his Word a reality in your life? Are you ready to feel a holy and empowered strength in your weakened spirit?

My prayer is that the Lord is slowly using this book to open your eyes and help you see, maybe for the very first time, the damage that your addiction to adrenaline, busyness, and/or stress may be having on you, your heart, your health, your faith, and your family. My hope is that you can sense Jesus reaching deep into the places of your spirit that nothing else has been able to reach and planting the seed for a compelling desire to change and be changed.

Psalm 38:9 says, "You know what I long for, Lord; you hear my every sigh." God already knows the longings of your heart. Take a moment and talk to him about them, remembering that, when you ask, you will receive.

Reflection Questions

1. Consider any situations or circumstances that have been causing you great stress. "Think of your most stressful circumstance right now and write it in the space below, and then answer the questions that follow. Use these questions as a thought provoking activity to help you tackle additional stressful situations you are facing as well."

A stressful situation or circumstance

_____

_____

_____

Ways you have dealt with this situation in the past

_____

_____

_____

Do you always hope for different results, even if you are continually addressing the problem in the same manner?

_____

_____

_____

Ways to approach this problem differently

_____

_____

_____

Benefits that may result from changing your reaction and/or action towards the issue

_____

_____

_____

Consequences of continuing in the same old ways that have not worked in the past.

_____

_____

_____

If you have been addressing the above issues in the same ways over and over again, while expecting or hoping for different results, pray for guidance on how to begin making different choices and asking God to give you the strength to change and the humility to rely on his power alone.

2. Is it possible that you are an adrenaline junkie? What category do you see yourself in: The Accomplisher, the Personal Deflector, the Deflector, or the Dramatist? If you are aware of some areas within yourself that you need to change, what actions can you take to make strides for personal improvement in those areas of weakness?

3. Are you too busy for your own good? What responsibilities do you currently hold that you can delegate to someone else to relieve some of the pressure you feel? If you are unsure, spend some time in prayer, asking for clarity about God's priorities for your life, or write your prayer below. Seek his will about what things you should be devoting your time to and what you should let go of.

4. Have you ever asked God to rescue your heart and refresh your spirit? If not, what has prevented you from doing that?

5. If you have asked God for "rescue" in the past and he intervened in your life in divine ways, jot down your memories of that experience. Tuck these memories into your heart and allow them to be your motivation to turn your life and all your current stressors over to him today.

6. If you have never recognized the need to be rescued but now understand the power of God's intervention, write a personal prayer of humility and praise to God; express your need to be rescued, while committing to trust him with the situations in your life and asking for his power and strength to persevere.

7. Has there been a time when you knew that God's strength was the only reason you were able to make it through a serious adversity? How does knowing he is capable of holding you up equip you to face the issues you are facing today?

Stress Busting Scriptures

Those who know your name will trust in you,
for you, Lord, have never forsaken those who seek you.

Psalm 9:10 NIV

In you our fathers put their trust; they trusted and you delivered them.
They cried to you and were saved;
in you they trusted and were not disappointed.

Psalm 22:4–5 NIV

Be very careful, then, how you live—not as unwise but as wise, making the
most of every opportunity, because the days are evil. Therefore do not be
foolish, but understand what the Lord's will is.

Ephesians 5:15–17 NIV

"Give justice to the poor and the orphan;
uphold the rights of the oppressed and the destitute.
Rescue the poor and helpless;
deliver them from the grasp of evil people."

Psalm 82:3–4

And this world is fading away, along with everything that people crave.
But anyone who does what pleases God will live forever.

1 John 2:17

Chapter Nine

Choose Your Weapons

People deal with stress in many different ways. Some people work off their stress by participating in sports or exercise, while others want to relax in a hot tub or sit in a sauna. Some take a relaxing vacation, while others snuggle up with a good book. But, unfortunately, far too many people turn to dangerous and even deadly choices in their desperate search for stress relief.

Many people turn to alcohol, caffeine, food, cigarettes, and illegal or prescription drugs when they find it impossible to find stress relief in any other way. It breaks my heart to see people so desperate for relief that they will do anything for it—especially when I know that all they really need is Jesus.

Regrettably, some people honestly believe that they can deal with their stress better if they have a few drinks every night to "take the edge off." Enjoying an alcoholic drink in the evenings has become a favorite past time in our society, but, when it becomes a necessity to deal with life, it becomes a threat to our health. Other people feel that eating will ease their stress and make them feel more relaxed, so they become consumed with filling themselves with food, hoping the comfort of food will sooth the emptiness they fill. Many others turn to drugs to help them either cope or forget, while telling themselves that their drug use is only "until things get better." But just like every lie the devil throws at us, succumbing to these falsehoods will only lead to more stress.

None of these methods bring permanent relief, yet all of them will exacerbate the problem. If people constantly seek out stress relief through bad choices, addictions in many forms can secretly begin to rear their ugly heads—which eventually brings on more stress and anxiety than they ever thought possible. The consequences of the addiction only compound all the stressors that were already present. Sadly enough, for people who have kicked their former habits of substance abuse or any harmful addictive behaviors, stress is one of the major factors known to cause a relapse, even after prolonged periods of abstinence.

There are so many worldly weapons available at our fingertips to help us win the war against stress, yet all are completely inadequate to fight the battles that life brings. When charging towards the giant of stress in our lives, we must choose our weapons for the battle very carefully.

Choose God

Wouldn't it be awesome if we could ask God for strength and immediately feel a physical, electrical infusion of spirituality, becoming instantly empowered with new energy and unshakable faith to face the days ahead? Maybe even transform into a superhero with superhuman strength in the blink of an eye? If God willed that to happen, it certainly would be incredible, but he usually chooses more subtle ways to intervene in our lives so that we can discover where true strength for the battle really comes from.

Real strength results from persistent communication and fellowship with him and allowing his words to guide us through each day. Just as David beat Goliath because he chose God as his weapon, we can choose God as our weapon of choice when facing battles of any kind.

Isaiah 40:31 says, "But those who trust in the Lord will find new strength. They will soar high on wings like eagles. They will run and not grow weary. They will walk and not faint." Fully trusting in the Lord is where we draw the kind of strength we need—that spiritual infusion of power that comes from daily devotion to biblical principles. It is this constant connection with God that will enable us to be transformed and empowered by him. How can we continue to feel stressed if we are transformed and empowered in Christ? Think about it.

So what does spiritual strength actually look like? In our egocentric society, we typically consider strength to be a physical attribute characterized by bulging muscles and a toned body. Movies of today reinforce this mindset, constantly portraying humans with inhuman strength as the only ones who have the power to initiate change, impact lives, or do good deeds. But, in God's opinion, this is an extremely distorted view.

Let's imagine God had a camera and began taking pictures of people who were pillars of strength in his eyes. What types of snapshots do you think he would take? I can imagine him capturing a shot of a mother on her knees every morning, pouring out her heart and pleading for him to protect her children as they grow up in our broken society.

I can see God taking a picture of a man in a high-rise office building going against the majority to stand up for ethics and integrity, despite whether negative consequences to his career may follow.

I can see God photographing a pastor in the pulpit, or on a street corner, encouraging anyone within earshot to embrace God's grace and love; a family staring at the smoldering remnants of their home, trusting that God will provide for them in the coming days; a teenager deciding to not give in to peer pressure because he made a vow of purity to God; a couple trying to forgive each other, just as Christ forgave them, as they work through the difficulties in their marriage; a husband fighting his temptation to view pornography by spending time in God's Word and asking God for the willpower to control lustful desires; a divorced woman surrendering her anger and bitterness towards her ex-husband, while rediscovering a peace and joy that had escaped her heart; or a man who loves his family so much that he works three jobs without resentment, thanking God for these opportunities to provide for those he loves.

I can only imagine that God would have a phenomenal heavenly photo album packed with pictures—beautiful pictures of infinite scores of his children who are exhibiting spiritual strength during the most trying times, with each and every one making him one very proud Daddy.

Ask yourself this question: If God really did have a camera, would he consider you picture worthy as someone who finds strength in him? If your answer is no, will you choose him today? If your answer is yes, then say "cheese."

Choose God's Word

I found myself in a dark field in the middle of the night, yet I was not alone. Although I could sense the presence of other people scattered throughout the field, I could not see them clearly because the only light was coming from a few slivers of moonbeams that crept across the acres. When I looked up, I saw a figure hovering near me. My eyes strained to try to make sense of what I was seeing.

This figure, along with all the others roaming throughout the barren field, seemed to be the silhouette of a soldier exuding the odorless scent of control and power. Suddenly, deep in my soul, I felt an overwhelming sense of danger so thick it was as if I could reach out and touch it, although I had no idea what danger lurked in this unknown place.

Before I could comprehend what was going on, I was thrown to the ground with great force, landing hard on my back as my head hit the cold dirt. I felt the weight of one of the figures pinning me firmly to the ground with my arms pulled tightly across my chest, prohibiting me from fighting back or trying to defend myself.

I could feel the hatred spewing from its spirit and the presence of evil dripping from the empty face. As I heard the wails of the other people in the field, my mind was overcome with fear and confusion about what was happening. Then, in the midst of this heart-ripping struggle, I had a divine revelation, as if God's voice were echoing through the meadows, but only I could hear him.

I became acutely aware to the depths of my soul that God's Word was my only hope. Scripture was my only lifeline. His promises would protect me. His words held power over evil. I knew his sovereignty was my only chance in this battle against unseen forces.

As could only happen in the context of a dream, where anything is possible, my body instantly shrunk down to the size of a pencil. I wriggled out of this evil being's grip and flung myself onto the pages of an open Bible, which just happened to be lying in the tall grasses beside me.

I immediately reached over with both hands and grabbed a handful of pages by the corner. I began to roll with all my might, tearing the pages from the creases of the book, and wrapping myself tightly into the pages of God's Word, as if I were a caterpillar entombing itself in a cocoon.

Instantly, the faceless enemies retreated in fear. My spirit felt the evil leap from my presence and I was freed from its weight upon me. Then, as if nothing had occurred, all was quiet. My heart was beating quickly and my breathing was labored. Although I was shaken up and dismayed, I was left unharmed.

And then I awoke from the deep slumber that had been holding me captive in this nightmare and tried to wrap my mind around the very real war I had just been engaged in.

As I lay there, staring with blurry, tear-filled eyes into the pitch-black darkness of 3:00 A.M., my mind raced in every direction. My thoughts stumbled over each other, each one trying to be the first to figure out what had just happened. Although I knew I was safe and sound in my own warm bed, my husband sleeping quietly beside me, my heart felt ravaged by the battle between good and evil that I had just encountered in the deepest recesses of my mind.

In that fragile moment with God, as my nightmare still hung in the quietness of the air, I could do nothing else—but pray. I spent the next hour in deep conversation with Jesus, and my spirit was awakened to what this dream really meant. I don't claim to be a dream interpreter, but I knew this was a message from God.

It suddenly became crystal clear that my entire family and I had been engaged in a fierce battle of spiritual warfare. You see, the past year had been filled with one blow after another, piling stress upon stress upon more stress, but I had merely attributed it all to life and human mistakes instead of giving credit where credit was due. Credit the enemy would gladly accept.

The devil loves to cause trouble, which is evidenced by the troubles that he brought upon Job in the Bible. Job was a good man who trusted God. And, although God did not cause Job's troubles, he did allow the devil to, which ultimately proved Job's trust and devotion to God in spite of overwhelming adversity and loss. I certainly don't know whether God caused our troubles to teach us valuable lessons that we are still learning or whether he allowed the devil to cause them to test the faith and devotion of our family. But, either way, I had been feeling a little like Job might have felt. My losses seemed huge, my emotions were raw, and my heart had been hurting. I had been so focused on *why* we were suffering through all these adversities that I had neglected to think about *who* could get me through them or *how* God was going to mold our hardships to be for his glory.

So, in the middle of the night, when the house was silent and it was just me and my sweet Jesus, all the fears and hurts and longings of my heart overflowed onto his feet like never before. My thoughts poured out of my mind like rapid waters rushing over the rocks of a swollen river. Amid my pleas for mercy, compassion, and protection, I felt a sense of freedom drench my spirit.

It was a strange sensation—a lightness and a release, neither of which I had felt in a very long time. It was a peace that had been eluding me for months as my mind struggled with negative emotions and the stressful situations that had kept my heart in bondage. As I allowed my mind to be engulfed with God's love, I was overcome with gratefulness, and I felt compelled to ask him . . . why? Yet, this time, it was a different *why*. Why would he care so much about me? Why did I matter? Why would he go to such lengths to get my attention and to rescue me from this invisible battle? Why did he die for me? Why does he love his children so much? Why was I worth it?

The only answer is a love we cannot comprehend from the Father who will fight to the death for us. In fact, he already did, and, because of his sacrifice on the cross for our sins, we do not have to live in the bondage that stress and spiritual warfare try to keep us in.

Through my most subconscious, dream-induced thoughts, God opened my eyes to show me that I had been living as an oppressed woman. Oppressed by anger. Oppressed by frustration, discouragement, hopelessness, and busyness. Oppressed by stress.

I had fought the battle of stress before on many occasions, but this go-around had been different. It had been more personal. It had been more emotionally damaging. This time it had involved pain, heartache, anger, and resentment, as opposed to just busyness. It had become a fierce battle—one that I was slowly losing—as I trudged through each day, unknowingly carrying the weight of the enemy's oppression.

I had given the devil a foothold in my life because I had not fully relied on the strongest weapon of all in this war against the unseen— God's Word. As a result, I had not guarded my heart from the enemy's tactics. Proverbs 4:23 instructs us, "Guard your heart above all else, for it determines the course of your life." I now understand the importance of this command more than ever before.

During the months prior to this God-inspired dream, I had been harboring negative emotions from a circumstance in my life that was completely not my fault and completely out of my control. Although I knew God instructs us to trust in our faith, not in our feelings (Proverbs 3:5 says, "Trust in the Lord with all your heart; do not depend on your own understanding."), I was unaware of the toll my feelings had taken on my spirit. My feelings were running my life, or, should I say, ruining my life. Therefore, over a period of time, my negativity had erected an invisible wall that blocked my view of what God wanted to do in my life through my circumstances. A wall that blocked my view of seeing how much God loved me as my fears tried to convince me that he had abandoned me.

Most importantly, it was blocking my ability to find peace amid my chaos. Stress took on a whole new meaning, and I wasn't making time for quiet time with God.

I had temporarily and inadvertently allowed the frustrations to become my focus, instead of the life-saving promises of the Bible. So although my physical body was not actually at war with the unseen enemy as it was in my dream, my spiritual body was. And the time came for God to pry away the life-robbing grip the devil had around my throat. The time came for God to remind me that he does not leave his beloved ones to fight the battle alone. His Word, and all the truths tucked deep within every page and every verse, is the most powerful weapon that we have to fight this battle of stress.

Through this dream experience, God blessed me with a glimpse of the unseen spiritual battle that takes place every day in our spirits as a result of the damaging effects of stressful situations in our lives. He also blessed me with a reminder that, when life gets stressful, the devil gets crafty. We need to realize who the real enemies are. Ephesians 6:12 says, "For we are not fighting against flesh-and-blood enemies, but against evil rulers and authorities of the unseen world, against mighty powers in this dark world, and against evil spirits in the heavenly places."

Spiritual warfare is often a subject that people avoid for fear of being seen as "Jesus freaks" or religious fanatics. Or possibly because spiritual warfare is a hard subject to wrap our human minds around. But when our hearts are riddled with gaping holes from the battles we endure every day, I want you to know that the devil is most happy when you disregard his tactics as nothing more than tough luck. The enemy knows that if we don't acknowledge the invisible battle we are engaged in, we will not reach for the weapons that will bring us victory.

This battle is real, and it is stressful. It is a battle waged against us by the prince of this world through the adversities, circumstances, and heartaches we endure. It is a battle that keeps us busy and anxious so that our spirits will become weak and hopeless. It is a battle that we are hopeless to win unless we wrap ourselves in the promises and truths found on every single page of God's Word.

There is a battle going on for your mind and heart. You don't have to believe in spiritual warfare for the enemy to wage war on your life. In fact, he'd rather you not believe in it, because that makes his job much easier. But when it strikes, even when disguised as stress, you have the power within you and at your fingertips to fight it if you choose the right weapon.

Maybe you have felt unrest in your life lately, as I had. Maybe you have felt oppressed and distant from God but haven't been able to pry yourself free from negative memories or emotions holding your heart captive. Maybe you have been feeling confused and alone but unsure what steps to take to feel close to God again. Maybe your unwillingness to let go of anger or maybe unforgiveness has built a wall that you can no longer see over. Maybe you feel as if you are imprisoned by the stress that hovers over your life, with no glimmer of hope for relief. Or, just maybe, you have accidentally, gradually, and unknowingly given the devil a foothold in your heart because you failed to guard it above all else. God's desire is that you surrender all that is weighing you down. If you choose only one weapon to fight off your stress, let God's Word be it.

Choose Spiritual Vitamins

Last year, I experienced a serious tragedy. A hair tragedy, that is. In order to keep the gray hairs on my head at bay in the most cost-effective way, I had formed a monthly practice in my bathroom that involved some quality time with a box of Miss Clairol. One particular month, I got the great idea to try a slightly different color shade than usual in the hopes of brightening up my look, just a bit.

After purchasing my new hair color choice and returning back home, I opened the box, mixed up the contents, and pulled on the flimsy, loose, plastic gloves before applying the color to my clean locks. I followed up that treatment with a new self-highlighting kit that I had bought at the same time, thinking that a few highlights would give me a more trendy look.

After the allotted time period had passed, I showered, washed my hair, and wrapped a towel around my head as I went about the rest of my beauty routine. Then I stood in front of the mirror and removed the towel only to see an ugly, odd-colored mess sticking out from every direction. Pure panic set in, and, before you could say "hair color," I had put on a hat and was driving to the local drug store to get a new hair-color kit in my normal shade. But later that morning, when I applied the usual shade, my hair came out looking even worse since it was applied on top of that ugly, odd-colored mess to begin with.

Before my wet hair even had time to dry, I had an emergency appointment made at a local salon. I knew this was a problem that could only be solved by a professional. Upon arriving at the salon, I tried to ignore the look of shock on my hairdresser's face as I tried to come up with excuses for my crazy, at-home hair-coloring antics. But she held her tongue and sympathetically escorted me to her chair.

In an effort to find the best solution to the problem, she felt confident that applying highlights and lowlights would repair the unnamed color on my head and get my hair back to normal again. Although I hesitantly agreed with her decision (thinking this might cause even more damage than regular color), I trusted her expertise, pushed aside my concerns, and let her get to work.

When I left the salon I was somewhat pleased with the results. *At least,* I thought to myself, *I no longer looked like the perfect role model for the why-not-to-color-your-own-hair-at-home advertisement.* However, upon arriving home, my then eleven-year-old son took one look at my hair and exclaimed, "Mom, your hair looks like peanut butter and jelly." Gee . . . thanks, son.

We laughed, or maybe I should say my family all laughed at my expense as I tried to be gracious. But what he meant was that the highlights, although they were soft brown and caramel colored, and not tannish nutmeg and purple colored, looked like the peanut butter and jelly that comes swirled together in a jar. Nonetheless, it was not a compliment that I felt blessed to have received.

Several days passed and I was coping with my new hairstyle just fine—until my peanut butter and jelly hair began falling out. Apparently, all that over-processing had caused so much damage that the hair all over my head began breaking off in large chunks. Within a couple of weeks, I went from thick flowing hair down to my shoulders to an extremely short, chopped-up, multilayered hairdo. Although, calling it an actual "hairdo" is a stretch.

I immediately established a hate-hate relationship with my hair (at least with what was left of it). I toyed with the idea of calling my hairdresser and giving her a piece of mind, since I was sure at least that would make me feel better, even though my hair tragedy probably wasn't entirely her fault.

For months I mourned over my hair loss. I despised looking at myself in the mirror because my hair was simply hideous! I managed it the best I could and hoped for quick hair growth and repair. But nothing worked. The damage was done, and now I was left to live with the consequences of my decisions. I had to succumb to the reality that all the wishing and moaning in the world was not going to get my old hair back nor make it grow any faster.

After months of depression about my hair, waiting for it to grow back to no avail, I got desperate for a solution. When one of my daughters publicly announced that if I said how much I hated my hair one more time she would scream, I knew I had to do something to overcome this hair tragedy. So I went online and ordered some expensive hair vitamins and an overpriced hair-repair conditioning system. I decided to eat healthy and exercise more, because I had always heard those things helped to foster the growth and strength of hair and nails.

This stressful hair situation—coupled with my overly busy life as a mom, wife, volunteer, speaker, and writer—had left me feeling discouraged, exhausted, and fatigued. So, in addition to my hair vitamins, I purchased several general health vitamins, as well. I not only needed my hair back, I needed my energy back, too.

Little did I know that these vitamins would have more benefits than originally thought. I gradually began feeling more energetic and realized that my poor eating habits and lack of exercise had been affecting my stamina and zest for life. I noticed that my fingernails seemed longer and thicker. But the best news of all was that, even though it took over a year to reach a turning point, my pitiful hair slowly began to grow back!

Although doctors often encourage their patients to take vitamins for better overall health and quality of living, I just didn't expect the obvious and immediate results that came from a concentrated effort to be healthy. As I was relishing the fact that I had hair again and feeling much better as a whole, I was prompted to consider what other areas of my life might be in need of a boost. What other areas could benefit from new zest and energy? The first thing that came to my mind was my walk with Jesus. My faith was a priority in my life; however, it had become routine and regular, instead of extraordinary and passionate. The thought of getting a spiritual boost was exciting, so I began pondering the idea of "spiritual vitamins," making a list of ones that I could take advantage of right away.

The next day I started working through my list of ideas, with the first one being to call a few of my friends to lift me up in prayer. I knew if I was going to get intentional about boosting my relationship with Jesus that the devil would get intentional about preventing me from doing that. I was well aware that I would need to be bathed in prayer.

Next, I committed to reading my devotional each morning. I picked up a few new Christian book releases that were filled with encouragement from biblical principles. Most importantly, I began reading God's Word again every day and growing my hunger for my daily portion of him.

I allowed his whispers to speak to my spirit each time I came across verses or passages that I could apply to the circumstances I was facing (although feeling pretty sure that there were no verses in the Bible about hair repair). I sought out his peace in my heart when my days were far from peaceful. And I attended a few powerful worship experiences, which rejuvenated my spirit and reenergized my soul.

After a while I realized that I not only felt physically better, I felt spiritually better, as well. The spiritual vitamins I had been ingesting every day had improved my spiritual health. They had become my most recent weapons against stress, discouragement, and frustration, and they were helping me win the battle against the enemy who wanted me to feel defeated.

First Peter 2:2 says, "Like newborn babies, you must crave pure spiritual milk so that you will grow into a full experience of salvation. Cry out for this nourishment." Paul knew that in order to stay close to Christ and be equipped to handle the problems and stress that life would bring, we would need to be fed spiritually on a daily basis.

If you are hungering for not only stress relief but also a renewed spirit and a healthier outlook on life, cry out for the nourishment that God provides. Consider taking some spiritual vitamins in the coming months and allow God to feed your soul. Just as tangible vitamins will improve your physical health, spiritual vitamins are guaranteed to improve your spiritual health. And, trust me, you will be amazed at the benefits you will reap—and maybe even in your hair and nails, if you're lucky. Just kidding.

Choose Prayer

I believe in the power of prayer. It is not just a religious duty, it is a spiritual privilege knowing that we are not just talking to God, but with God, and expecting to hear his reply. In David's prayer in Psalm 86, he begins by asking God to hear his pleas for protection, grace, and joy: "Bend down, O Lord, and hear my prayer; answer me, for I need your help. Protect me, for I am devoted to you. Save me, for I serve you and trust you. You are my God. Be merciful to me, O Lord, for I am calling on you constantly. Give me happiness, O Lord, for I give myself to you. O Lord, you are so good, so ready to forgive, so full of unfailing love for all who ask for your help. Listen closely to my prayer, O Lord; hear my urgent cry" (vv. 1–6). Then in the following verse, he acknowledges that he knows God will answer: "I will call to you whenever I'm in trouble, and you will answer me" (v. 7).

David admits his imperfections and his concerns and asks for God's intervention. Although David often wavered in making good decisions, he never wavered in believing that God loved him despite his sin. He was confident that God heard his prayers, and he was confident that God would respond to them. David's hope was in God, and ours must be too.

As believers, if we doubt whether God hears and will respond to our prayers, then we need to question whether we truly believe, because Scripture clearly states that God hears our prayers. For example, Hebrews 4:16 says, "So let us come boldly to the throne of our gracious God. There we will receive his mercy, and we will find grace to help us when we need it most." However, though God always hears the prayers of those who believe in him, he may not always answer in the way we would like. He may say yes to our requests, or he may say no; it all depends on whether what we ask for aligns with his perfect will. He always knows what we need better than we do. And I have learned the hard way that what we want or desire can often be completely different from what we need.

Maybe you have not chosen prayer as a weapon lately because you wonder if God really hears. If so, I want to assure you that he does—not because I said so, but because God did. All throughout the Bible we are reassured that God does hear our prayers. One other example is found in Psalm 34:15: "The eyes of the LORD watch over those who do right; his ears are open to their cries for help."

Prayer is a weapon that nobody can ever take away from us, not even our worst enemy. It is a powerful and private conversation between us and the Sovereign Creator in which no one can intervene. If you have been struggling with prayer and believing that God hears every word you think or speak, I encourage you to consider verse 11 from David's prayer in Psalm 86: "Teach me your ways, O LORD, that I may live according to your truth! Grant me purity of heart, so that I may honor you."

Even David knew that life was full of distractions, so he prayed for an undivided mind. He knew that, when life got hard, he might be tempted to focus on things other than God; so he prayed for the ability to live in God's ways and the strength to stay focused in his mind and heart.

Prayer works, and it is a weapon that God calls us to use without ceasing.

Choose Victory

One day, during my quiet time with God, I came across the verses of Psalm 89:9–10, which say, "You rule the oceans. You subdue their storm-tossed waves. You crushed the great sea monster. You scattered your enemies with your mighty arm."

As I read this verse again, I began to ponder the idea of an actual sea monster. Since when are there sea monsters of biblical proportions lurking about in the oceans? I thought those were only found in science-fiction movies. The whole concept seemed beyond my understanding, yet here it was in God's infallible Word.

So, with my curiosity peaked, I began to research this unfamiliar verse and the existence of "sea monsters." I began my study by looking up this same verse in the NIV Bible, which translates the verse, "You crushed Rahab like one of the slain." This translation gave a name to the mysterious sea monster—Rahab (not to be confused with the prostitute in the book of Joshua).

I also discovered that in Hebrew the name Rahab portrayed a mythical sea monster that represented chaos and stress and was referred to as the demonic angel of the sea. According to the *Holman Illustrated Bible Dictionary*, the word "chaos" is referred to throughout Scripture and is considered to be a state of being that is completely opposite of what God stands for. The Holman definition of Rahab went on to explain that:

> In ancient Semitic legends, a terrible chaos-monster was called Rahab (the proud one), or Leviathan (the twisting dragon-creature), or Yam (the roaring sea). While vehemently denouncing idolatry and unmistakably proclaiming the matchless power of the One Almighty God, biblical writers did not hesitate to draw upon these prevalent pagan images to add vividness and color to their messages, trusting that their Israelite hearers would understand the truths presented.

God demonstrated His power in creation graphically in the crushing defeat of chaos. He quieted the sea, shattering Rahab, making the heavens fair, and piercing the fleeing serpent (Job 26:12–13). His victory over Leviathan (*another mythical creature*) is well-known (Job 41:1–8; Isa. 27:1); Leviathan and the sea are at His command (Ps. 104:26). In creation He curbed the unruly sea and locked it into its boundaries (Job 38:1–11). He stretched out the heavens and trampled the back of Yam, the sea (Job 9:8).

A second use of the chaos-monster figure involved God's victories at the time of the exodus, using the term Rahab as a nickname for Egypt. Through His power God divided the sea and crushed Leviathan (Ps. 74:13–14). He calmed the swelling sea and smashed Rahab like a carcass (Ps. 89:9–10). By slaying the monster Rahab, God allowed the people to pass through the barrier sea (Isa. 51:9–10). Mockingly, Isaiah called Egypt a helpless, vain Rahab whom God exterminated (Isa. 30:7). The psalmist anticipated the day when Rahab and Babylon would be forced to recognize God's rule (Ps. 87:4). In Ezek. 29:3; 32:2, the Pharaoh of Egypt is called the river monster that will be defeated at God's will. [26]

What I realized was that Rahab is not really a sea creature at all, but instead the portrayal of a being that possesses ungodly and evil qualities. Although Rahab is referenced with regards to Egypt in particular, it represents the chaos that is present in all of our lives. The Bible uses the concept of sea monsters, or mighty beasts, as a metaphor for the prideful rebellion of all people against God's ways.

Another bible study website I visited had this to say:

In the Canaanite world, Rahab was a mythical coiling sea-monster, slain by Baal in the primordial chaos. Biblically, Rahab is used as a symbol of Egypt. Metaphorically, the nation is a monster in the chaos of the sea of nations. While Rahab the sea monster occurs six times in the Hebrew Old Testament, it doesn't always come through clearly in the KJV, as the word is sometimes translated instead of being preserved as a name. The name Rahab means storm or arrogance and so when the KJV translates the word it uses English words like pride or the proud, though the KJV margin sometimes does make reference to the original.[27]

The association of Rahab with the sea or waters confirms the fact that it belongs to the sphere of evil. According to many references to the sea in Scripture, the sea is often a symbol of the forces of oppression and death, and Rahab seems to embody all of these qualities.

As I processed all of this information, I began to notice how many negative characteristics and sins that this one sea monster stood for: chaos, darkness, insolence, pride, storms, and arrogance. All of the things that lead to oppression and death. They are attributes that God sees as monstrous problems in a Christian's life. Problems that affect the soul, pull us apart from him, cause us to fret and worry, and eventually lead us into the raging sea of stress, with huge waves crashing down upon us.

Today, millions of people are drowning in the seas of a nation whose culture lives and thrives on chaos. For some, stress is a symbol of success—an outward example of how busy they are, thus exemplifying their importance. Their adrenaline addiction feeds the soul, resulting in pride and arrogance. For others, stress is simply a by-product of their own attitudes or of trying to control situations that are beyond their control. In any case, chaos, darkness, and hopelessness can result, and the outcome is not a pretty picture for anyone.

Yet, when I skimmed through the six verses about Rahab in the Old Testament, I noticed one important and comforting commonality. Read over these verses and see if you notice it as well:

And God does not restrain his anger. Even the monsters of the sea are crushed beneath his feet. So who am I, that I should try to answer God or even reason with him? (Job 9:13–14)

The foundations of heaven tremble; they shudder at his rebuke. By his power the sea grew calm.By his skill he crushed the great sea monster. His Spirit made the heavens beautiful, and his power pierced the gliding serpent. These are just the beginning of all that he does, merely a whisper of his power. Who, then, can comprehend the thunder of his power? (Job 26:11–14)

I will record Rahab and Babylon among those who acknowledge me—Philistia too, and Tyre, along with Cush—and will say, "This one was born in Zion." (Ps. 87:4 NIV)

Who is like you, LORD God Almighty? You, LORD, are mighty, and your faithfulness surrounds you. You rule over the surging sea; when its waves mount up, you still them. You crushed Rahab like one of the slain; with your strong arm you scattered your enemies. (Ps. 89:8–10 NIV)

This message came to me concerning the animals in the Negev: The caravan moves slowly across the terrible desert to Egypt— donkeys weighed down with riches and camels loaded with treasure—all to pay for Egypt's protection. They travel through the wilderness, a place of lionesses and lions, a place where vipers and poisonous snakes live.

All this, and Egypt will give you nothing in return. Egypt's promises are worthless! Therefore, I call her Rahab— the Harmless Dragon. (Isa. 30:6–7)

Awake, awake, arm of the LORD, clothe yourself with strength! Awake, as in days gone by, as in generations of old. Was it not you who cut Rahab to pieces, who pierced that monster through? Was it not you who dried up the sea, the waters of the great deep, who made a road in the depths of the sea so that the redeemed might cross over? (Isa. 51:9–10 NIV)

Did you see the commonality with each reference to the demon of chaos? God rules.

He rules over everything and always prevails. It may seem that our chaos, magnified by stress and busyness and worry, is ruling over our lives, but if God is ruling over our hearts, victory is possible. But we do have to choose to believe in his sovereignty if we want to enjoy the victory that he offers.

So why do most of us search everywhere for stress relief, except God? Why do we reach for every weapon available, except the Bible? Why do we spend time searching for something, or someone, that can save us from these sea monsters in our own hearts when God is only a prayer away? Why do we live out every day as if there is no hope to overcome our chaos and no possibility for living a stressed-less life when Scripture repeatedly reassures us that God has the power and the peace to make that happen?

The answer is simple—in the same way we may feel that prayer doesn't work, we may not believe that God is powerful enough to slay the monsters in our lives or handle our problems, so we resolve to live in a sea of despair and stress. As we neglect to reach for God's help, we end up being pulled deeper into the abyss where more invisible monsters of chaos await us in the darkness.

But in Psalm 89:9–10 especially, God's triumph over Rahab is made crystal clear. He rules over all. He has the power to calm the storms in your life. He has the sovereignty to crush the inner demons you are battling against. He always has victory over the enemy, and he has already won the battle. He always has been, is, and always will be triumphant.

God can effortlessly still the brutal waves in the raging sea of our lives, but we have to put our lives in his hands before he can do so. No monster is too powerful for the All Powerful.

You may be fully aware of some of the monsters lurking in your heart that are stealing your joy and keeping you shackled with stress. But, if not, ask God to reveal to you what those monsters are and then turn those monsters over to him. Let God take over the battle for you. And then take a deep breath and rest in knowing that he will have victory, in his perfect timing and in his perfect ways, if you give him a chance to go to battle for you.

If you are searching for a weapon to fight your stress, don't look to the ways of the world. Don't allow the devil to fill your head with lies that drugs, alcohol, physical pleasures, or random coping mechanisms are the only choices you have. Choose God, his Word, prayer, and spiritual vitamins. As you fight the battle with these tools, you will also be simultaneously choosing your victory.

◌ Reflection Questions

1. Ponder the thought of spiritual warfare with regards to any difficult situations you have been struggling with lately. Have you considered that these adversities could be spiritual warfare, rather than "tough luck"? Ask God to provide you with spiritual clarity. Take some time to research God's Word along with Bible commentaries to obtain a deeper understanding of the enemy's ways so that you can be more aware and better spiritually prepared for the enemy's attacks in the future. Jot down any notes or thoughts here.

2. Make a list of "spiritual vitamins" that you can begin taking to help give your spiritual walk with God a boost. Consider things like more fellowship with other believers, attending church more regularly, going to revivals and new Bible studies, and making time for daily devoted quiet time, focused prayers, daily online devotionals, and so on. Put them in order of priority to you, and commit to start taking at least one new vitamin this week.

3. What does spiritual strength mean to you? After you define spiritual strength from your perspective, list a few ways that you have exhibited spiritual strength in difficult situations in the past. Write a brief prayer, praising God for helping you get through those situations in his strength.

4. If God were to take a snapshot of you right now, what would his picture show? List a few adjectives that might describe your photo, even if they are not positive descriptives. (Be sure to use this as a self-assessment, a tool that will push you towards a goal of spiritual growth, not as a list of reasons to practice self-condemnation.)

5. Now consider what you would like for God's picture of you to look like. Write down the strengths or positive attributes that you want God to help you develop.

6. If the picture of your reality is not a picture of God's strength working within you, how can you begin making some positive changes to build your dependence and trust in God? What situations or issues do you need to turn over to God, humbly admitting that you don't have the strength to persevere without him?

7. Do you have any monsters lurking in your heart? Write down the first things that come to mind. Take time to turn them over to God, asking him to bring victory over those monsters and convert your heart from one with a spirit of fear to a spirit of victory.

Stress Busting Scriptures

The LORD is my light and my salvation—whom shall I fear?
The LORD is the stronghold of my life—of whom shall I be afraid?

Psalm 27:1 NIV

God is our refuge and strength, an ever-present help in trouble.

Psalm 46:1b NIV

"Do not be afraid, for I have ransomed you. I have called you by name; you are mine. When you go through deep waters, I will be with you. When you go through rivers of difficulty, you will not drown. When you walk through the fire of oppression, you will not be burned up; the flames will not consume you. For I am the LORD, your God, the Holy One of Israel, your Savior."

Isaiah 43:1b–3a

The God of peace will soon crush Satan under your feet.
May the grace of our Lord Jesus be with you.

Romans 16:20

Be on guard. Stand firm in the faith. Be courageous. Be strong.

1 Corinthians 16:13

Chapter Ten

Broken for Breakthrough

Most of us desperately want to feel capable of handling the trials and problems of life on our own. We want to feel equipped to deal with what life throws at us, and we take pride in accomplishments of doing so. But it is often that exact determination and pride that causes unnecessary stress. In fact, some of us would rather risk falling flat on our faces than admit we need help.

When we get caught up in this battle of wills, God sometimes allows us to get to our breaking point before he steps in, and he does it for our own benefit. Until we recognize that we are utterly helpless on our own, we will not be able to understand that we really have no control over life. Our pain and suffering will serve as a catapult to drive us towards God, and, when we begin to see him, our hope will be renewed.

One great example of finding hope when we least expect it is found in 1 Kings 17, where we learn of a widow who was broken and had lost all hope. In this chapter, the Prophet Elijah was told by God to take a trip to Zarephath in the region of Sidon, and God promised that he would provide for his needs while he was gone. In keeping with his Word as he always does, God divinely arranged for a widow to supply Elijah's food and housing needs when he reached Zarephath.

Upon arriving at Zarephath, although he did not know for sure that this was part of God's plan and provision for him, Elijah saw the widow picking up sticks and asked her for some food. In 1 Kings 17:12, the widow replied to Elijah by saying, "As surely as the LORD your God lives . . . I don't have any bread—only a handful of flour in a jar and a little oil in a jug. I am gathering a few sticks to take home and make a meal for myself and my son, that we may eat it—and die" (NIV).

Is it just me or does that sound just a bit overly dramatic—like something a teenager would say if she was told she couldn't go out with her friends on Friday night? "Mom, if I don't get to go, I might die!" The widow's reply sounds borderline drama queen, yet also a tad sarcastic, but I feel sure that, in either case, it was not the response Elijah expected. In thinking about this, I began to wonder what tone she actually used when making this statement to Elijah.

Maybe she said it with great bitterness and anger in her heart, shaking her fist at God, wondering why he had let her husband die—leaving both her and her son without food. Maybe she said it with sarcasm, knowing that she probably would not really die after her next meal, but life was such a struggle that she would not care either way. Maybe she was just being honest, knowing that their malnutrition was growing worse and honestly believing that any meal could potentially be their last. Or maybe she said it in great despair, with her head hung low, tears falling from her eyes, full of hopelessness and sadness, not wanting to die but seeing no way out. And since no solution seemed within her reach, she had already surrendered to that imminent fate.

We have no idea how this poor woman was really feeling, but what we *do* know is that God had not forgotten her. He knew she was in the deepest stress of her life. And, although she probably thought God did not care about her situation, he had already made plans for her miracle to occur in his perfect timing.

1 Kings 17:13–16 reads:

Elijah said to her, "Don't be afraid. Go home and do as you have said. But first make a small cake of bread for me from what you have and bring it to me, and then make something for yourself and your son. For this is what the LORD, the God of Israel, says: 'The jar of flour will not be used up and the jug of oil will not run dry until the day the LORD gives rain on the land.'"

She went away and did as Elijah had told her. So there was food every day for Elijah and for the woman and her family. For the jar of flour was not used up and the jug of oil did not run dry, in keeping with the word of the LORD spoken by Elijah. (NIV)

Even though this woman's circumstances seemed grim, causing her to lose all hope of getting out of the pit that she had found herself in, which was of no fault of her own, God had a plan. He had ordained that Elijah meet this widow at an appointed day and time. And, as she carried out her routine tasks, just like any other day, God put his plan, her miracle, into place.

We are not told in this Scripture that the widow had been seeking God's intervention. In fact, we could safely assume that she did not know the Lord, since, when she spoke to Elijah, she made the comment in verse 12, "As surely as the LORD *your* God lives. . . ." Notice she didn't say "my God," but instead she referred to God as the Lord of Elijah. Conversely, she probably worshiped the idol Baal. But the Lord still saw her suffering and cared about her nonetheless. Despite what some people tend to believe, God truly does love and shows himself to all people because he wants every person to put their faith in him (Matt. 5:45).

God also reiterates his love for all people in Romans 2:4, where it says, "Don't you see how wonderfully kind, tolerant, and patient God is with you? Does this mean nothing to you? Can't you see that his kindness is intended to turn you from your sin?" God is merciful and loving to all people, whether they believe in him or not, yet his desire is that all will come to know him through this mercy. And sometimes he uses stressful situations to help them do that.

God was kind to the widow and provided for her physical, emotional, and spiritual needs. He eliminated the physical sources of stress in her life (finances and food) and provided a spiritual source of strength by allowing her to witness miracles, through Elijah, but that only God could do.

Maybe you can relate to the feelings that the widow expressed to Elijah. When faced with overwhelming despair and stress, it is normal to feel hopeless and defeated, wondering what tomorrow holds—or whether there will even be a tomorrow. But I urge you to focus on the truth despite what you are going through. And the truth is that God has a miracle planned for you too, if you are willing to expect it, look for it, and wait for it to play out in God's perfect timing.

If you are in a pit of stress or despair, don't succumb to defeat. Don't accept that difficult place as your fate. Even though God has allowed you to be there right now, he never intended for you to live there. Our God is bigger than whatever problem you are facing. The only way to see past the problem is to believe that he has not forgotten or abandoned you and that, at the exact time that he has ordained, he will reach down and pick you up.

Just as a mother would never forget her own child, our God never forgets his children. And even if you have not been looking for him, he has been looking for you.

Miracles in the Pit

Let's take one quick last look at that season of my life when I had found myself in a deep cavern of overwhelming stress, before deciding to leave my corporate position.

My job environment had reached an unbearable point, making me feel a bit like that widow wondering whether she could make it through another dreadful day. The overwhelming and unrelenting stress and the personal and emotional attacks that my unkind boss barraged me with had continuously worsened. It seemed that, the harder I tried to do my very best, the harder things became. No matter how much I accomplished, it was never enough. The more I tried to succeed, the more I seemed to fail in the eyes of someone with unreasonable expectations of perfection. I was spinning my wheels—doing the same thing over and over but expecting different results. All the while, I was losing my sanity one day at a time.

Just like the widow picking up sticks, I was carrying great despair in my heart. I had allowed one person to completely destroy my self-confidence. And, although I desperately wanted my circumstances to be different, it seemed completely out of my control to change them. On really bad days, my alter ego, Miss Drama Queen, would escape from her dark cave. I would find myself thinking much like that widow, convinced that the stress and anxiety was going to kill me and I would surely die after my next meal, too.

But, in addition to my husband's income, my family needed my income to survive. Our lifestyle was built on two incomes and the idea of trying to survive on one income seemed farfetched, absurd, and, frankly, a bit terrifying. I was convinced that, if I quit my job, my pantry would consistently be as empty as the shelves in the widow's home. As a result, I felt powerless and hopeless. I had accepted my fate of being doomed to live in this pit of despair.

But I didn't want to accept it.

In my heart of hearts, I knew that there had to be more to life than what I was experiencing. I simply could not force myself to believe that God's plan for my life was the one I was living—a life so void of joy and so full of stress.

After months of prayer, it became painfully clear that I was obviously *not* where God wanted me to be. I was *not* doing what God had planned for my life. I was *not* living in his will. I began to pray fervently for God to rescue me from my situation and from my stress, in whatever way he chose.

Over the coming weeks, I began to figure out the root of the real problem, and I didn't like what I saw. God opened my eyes to see that he had not forgotten or abandoned me—it was I who had forgotten him. Although I was still reading his Word and trying to be in his will in my thoughts and behaviors, I was still living in disobedience. Although I was serving as a leader in women's ministry at my home church, I was still deliberately refusing to do as he had asked me years ago in the sanctuary, where his voice had echoed through my heart.

It was I who had allowed his call to *go and share* to become a distant memory. The real problem was revealed: I was living out the consequences of the life I had chosen, instead of enjoying the plans he had intended for me. I had only myself and my lack of faith to blame.

After one particularly rough week in the office, after having spent several days licking my emotional wounds, I found myself crying huge tears as I endured my miserable hour-long rush hour commute across town to my office. I dreaded the thought of another stressful, unrewarding, and draining day. And the nervous stomach and splitting headache were already making their morning debut.

I arrived at my building, parked my car, and shut off the ignition. Instead of getting out of the car, I just sat there staring aimlessly out of the window at the sea of cars lined up neatly in the dark hollows of the parking deck. My spirit was crushed, and my motivation to work was gone. I bowed my head, tears still pouring, and pleaded with God for mercy. I held nothing back; I laid my deepest feelings at his feet. *Oh Jesus, I am in a deep, dark, bottomless pit. At the end of my rope. I need you. I am desperate for a change—desperate to see you at work in my life. Do you remember me? Do you see me? Do you still love me Lord? Am I acceptable in your eyes? Will you forgive me for my disobedience? Help me. Save me from this abyss that I have fallen into.*

The last words I uttered in my prayer were these: *Lord, what would you have me do? Please make your will known to me, and I will follow, no matter what. Is it possible for me to resign and stay at home with my precious children? My heart longs to stay home, but is it possible that you are calling me to leave this job, and trust you to provide for us financially? Is it possible that you have better plans for my life? Please Lord, please show me what I am to do.*

I was confused and distraught, having never felt at such a low point in my life. I was completely and absolutely broken. And it was exactly that state of brokenness that opened the door for God to finally give me a breakthrough.

Upon saying amen, I dried my tears, reapplied my makeup, and tried to gain my composure before making my way up to the twenty-third floor. I plopped down in my chair, downhearted and discouraged, and half-heartedly turned on my computer.

As had been the case for five years, my daily Proverbs 31 Ministries "Encouragement for Today" devotional (which I had signed up for after that infamous day at the women's seminar) greeted my eyes at the top of my inbox. And just as I did every morning, I began to read through the devotion, hoping to glean some encouragement to carry me through the day, but definitely not expecting a life-changing holy encounter.

When God Sends an E-mail

As I read the words in the devotion, my heart skipped a beat, my jaw dropped, and my eyes shot wide open in utter disbelief.

Read this excerpt from that morning's devotion, written by Glynnis Whitwer, senior editor of the *P31Woman* magazine:

> It was a warm autumn night as I watched my sons practice football. Three other mothers and I lounged in our chairs, alternately glancing at the practice to make sure we saw the tackles and passes, and discussing the frustration of preparing dinner on busy weeknights.
>
> As we talked a bit more, I discovered that all three of them worked full-time outside their homes. These devoted moms really wanted to prepare nutritious meals, but it was all they could do to race home from work, grab a quick snack and then race to practice. After practice, they returned home exhausted and grabbed another snack item.
>
> When the conversation turned to me, I shared that because I work part-time from home I was able to make an early dinner. After that, each lady expressed her desire to be home during the day, and in almost the same breath, declared why she couldn't do it. My heart broke with compassion because I saw the sense

of helplessness in their words and facial expressions. It was as if they were resigned to a full-time job, and that was that.

My three football-practice friends are like hundreds of thousands of women across the country who wish they could stay home but don't think it's possible. All they see is one obstacle after another. They see a mountain of debt, the problem of health insurance, a child's empty college fund, an unsupportive spouse or a workplace that "needs" them.

What these women don't see is a God who can handle all those obstacles. Instead of trusting God to provide, they work harder and longer to make ends meet. But the ends just get farther apart.

Psalm 20:7 says, "Some trust in chariots and some in horses, but we trust in the name of the LORD our God." Although that was written thousands of years ago, I wonder if we sometimes underestimate God's capabilities and trust in our own "horses" and "chariots." We may have a head-knowledge about trusting God, but in reality, we trust in a company, our physical strength, or our intelligence.

The last sentence of the devotion brought me to my knees. It read like this: "I've found that sometimes God waits for us to make the first move, believing that he will take care of us. . . . Is God asking you to trust him today? Is he saying to you, 'I've heard your cries; I know you want to be home. It's now time for you to move on and make it happen.'"[28]

Did you notice the irony of that last sentence? It was as if I was reading my own prayer in written form—the prayer that still lingered in the thick, humid air in the parking deck beneath me. I sat at my desk literally stunned, and the tears became uncontrollable. I had the sensation of my breath being taken away as I processed the thought that the Author and Creator of the Universe—the Holy Sovereign God, Elohim, Adonai, Jehovah, El Roi, El Shaddai, Abba, Heavenly Father, Christ Jesus—had heard my prayer that morning, and I had tangible evidence of his answer staring at me in typed, black letters.

In that moment, in a very ordinary office, I was extraordinarily transformed from a hopeless, broken soul to a hopeful, whole young woman who had experienced a life-changing breakthrough out of her brokenness. God had let me go my own way, but when I was ready to be rescued, he showed up with flying colors.

Psalm 34:17–18 tells us, "The LORD hears his people when they call to him for help. He rescues them from all their troubles. The LORD is close to the brokenhearted; he rescues those whose spirits are crushed." These verses shower us with a powerful reminder of how close the Lord is, even when we feel crushed, brokenhearted, or stressed. He truly wants to rescue us. Despite how far down we feel we have sunk or how deep we have sunk into a pit of stress or hopelessness, our prayers will always reach his holy ears. And he will answer.

I have come to understand that God cannot use people greatly until he has broken them deeply. And when we embrace our brokenness, we are ready for breakthrough.

✍ Reflection Questions

1. In what ways can you relate to the widow in Zarephath? Are you experiencing any of the hopelessness or despair that she was feeling? Explain any commonalities you share.

2. Are you at your breaking point right now? Do you feel like you are in the lowest pit of your life, unsure how to climb your way out? What has caused you to feel this way?

3. Do you really believe that God still performs miracles, even in the twenty-first century? What are some examples of miracles or supernatural intervention that you have witnessed recently, whether big or small, in your life or someone else's?

4. How does acknowledging God's ability to still perform miracles help your faith to be stronger?

5. Why do you think God needs you to be completely broken before he can deliver a breakthrough? Explain your feelings, and ask God to help you begin looking at your future from his perspective.

6. Have you ever felt God calling you to a special purpose but were too afraid or insecure to move forward? Is it possible that some of your stress may be a result of choosing your own path instead of following God's?

If God placed a dream or call on your heart that you have ignored, jot it down in the margin as a reminder to pray for God's will and direction in the coming weeks. Pray for him to help you trust in his ways instead of your own and to have a faith that is stronger than your human fears or concerns.

7. Are you willing to admit that you are broken and embrace your brokenness so that you can experience a breakthrough? Write a brief prayer to God acknowledging your need for his intervention in your life and asking him to make his presence known in ways that you will feel and see.

Stress Busting Scriptures

A cheerful heart is good medicine,
but a crushed spirit dries up the bones.

Proverbs 17:22 NIV

He heals the brokenhearted and binds up their wounds.

Psalm 147:3 NIV

Whether you turn to the right or to the left,
your ears will hear a voice behind you, saying,
"This is the way; walk in it."

Isaiah 30:21 NIV

Dear brothers and sisters, when troubles come your way,
consider it an opportunity for great joy.

James 1:2

All praise to God, the Father of our Lord Jesus Christ.
It is by his great mercy that we have been born again,
because God raised Jesus Christ from the dead.
Now we live with great expectation.

1 Peter 1:3

Chapter Eleven

The Reset Button

We all get stuck in ruts from time to time and find ourselves in situations that we want out of. In fact, we have all probably felt like the widow with the sticks, like David facing Goliath, or like Hannah facing infertility and verbal persecution, even though our circumstances may have been entirely different. There is no doubt about it—we have all found ourselves in a pit at one time or another.

In this world of chaos, stress, and busyness we live in, it's easy to get off track and be pulled onto a path we would have never deliberately chosen. In many cases, we may even fall into a pit that we never saw coming because the twists and turns of life blinded us to the potential dangers ahead. Or we may have seen the all the warning signs that danger was ahead but failed to steer ourselves away from it and ended up driving smack into a brick wall.

In any case, when we find ourselves at the end of our rope, it's safe to say we probably all secretly wish we had a reset button for our lives, allowing us the opportunity to go back in time and make better decisions about the paths we have taken.

Although there is no official reset button, there are things we can do—beginning with choosing the right weapons and making Christ our priority—to "reboot" our lives and jump-start the process of getting back on track to a life that is filled with peace and joy.

Here are six action items that, if you are willing to implement them in your every day life, will serve as crucial stepping stones towards achieving your goal of living a stressed-less life.

1. Realign Your Life

Your word is a lamp to guide my feet and a light for my path.

Psalm 119:105

All too often our Bibles are nothing more than a pretty book that sits on the coffee table collecting dust. We may carry it back and forth to church, but we don't really consider it a resource tool for living. But what if we realigned our lives according to God's Word? What if we began to consider the Bible our only lifeline? What if we gave it the importance it actually deserved? Would our lives be different?

When pondering these questions for myself, I remembered a meaningful encounter that I experienced with my son right after he turned six years old.

Every year my church gives out Bibles to the rising first graders during a special part of the worship service set aside to recognize them. When this designated Sunday finally arrived, Michael was beaming with excitement. He could not wait to receive his very own special Bible.

Our children's minister began calling out the names of children one by one, and each child excitedly skipped down to the front of the church to accept his or her new Bible. My son sat there quietly, anxiously awaiting the sound of his name, and, when it was called, he jumped up, looked straight at me, and gave me a huge ear-to-ear grin. You would have thought he had won tickets to Disney World based on the joy on his little face!

He was handed his crisp new Bible, and then he skipped back to the pew where we were sitting. For the next thirty minutes, as the pastor shared his message, Michael admired his Bible. He held it close to him. He hugged it lovingly. He caressed it. He flipped through all the pages looking for pictures of the Bible stories he recognized. He smelled the fresh, crisp pages. He even kissed it over and over with silly little head-bobbing motions. He was so proud of and in love with his new Bible!

At home later that afternoon, he picked up his Bible and said to me with great emphasis and awe, with eyes wide open, "Mom, did you know that I have *God's. Holy. Word.* right in my hands?"

My motherly heart melted. As I witnessed a passion for Jesus in the heart of a child, I felt a twinge of guilt spread over my spirit—I considered how long it had been since I treasured God's Word that passionately. My son reminded me just how precious God's Word should be to us. Although he was too young at that time to fully understand all the lessons that the Bible teaches us, he knew in his innocent little heart that it was invaluable.

If only life could stay as simple as it was when we were six years old. With growth comes problems, and stress. And with all those stumbling blocks, we fall out of God's Word, allowing our lives to get off track and out of alignment.

Consider whether your life is aligned with the Word of God, and ask God to show you where changes need to be made. Time spent with God is always time well spent—so set a goal to get realigned.

2. Recognize Your Need

May your mercy come quickly to meet us, for we are in desperate need.

Psalm 79:8b NIV

Why is it that we so often have to be at the end of our rope before we feel desperate enough to call for help? Just as stress is a disease that takes its toll on our overall existence, self-sufficiency syndrome is a disease of the heart, as well. This syndrome is characterized by our desire to handle everything on our own, afraid to show any sign of weakness or neediness to anyone, including God.

God never meant for us to be self-sufficient. Dependable, yes. Responsible, yes. Confident, yes. Self-sufficient, no.

John 15:5 says, "Yes, I am the vine; you are the branches. Those who remain in me, and I in them, will produce much fruit. For apart from me you can do nothing." Why do we try to do things on our own when God's Word explicitly states we cannot do anything apart from him? Ask God to be your strength and deliverer; commit to depending on him first, even when you think you can "do it all by yourself."

3. Adjust Your Focus

Have you never heard? Have you never understood? The LORD is the everlasting God, the Creator of all the earth. He never grows weak or weary. No one can measure the depths of his understanding.

Isaiah 40:28

When change becomes necessary, that change often needs to begin with getting in focus. With respect to our faith walk, the time comes when we must take our focus off of our circumstances and put it on God.

I once heard my pastor say, "Trouble and adversity are like bananas—they come in bunches." This statement rings true—it always seems that when one stressful situation reaches the maximum level, another stressful situation falls in right behind it. Stress is higher during times of great adversity, but we have to deal with some level of stress every day.

When we focus on our circumstances instead of trusting God to work in our lives, we can become overwhelmed with worry and fear. We must allow God to fill our hearts with his peace. Remember that the Lord never grows weary, and he knows how to handle our problems much better than we do.

4. Be Filled with the Spirit

So I say, let the Holy Spirit guide your lives. Then you won't be doing what your sinful nature craves.

Galatians 5:16

The pull towards self-sufficiency can be strong. The temptation to worry can seem unbeatable. The longing to take control of a problem and absolve God from the privilege of intervening in our lives can become all-consuming. Yet, when we are filled with the Holy Spirit, we are empowered to stand firm against the pulls of the world.

If you have asked God to fill you with the Holy Spirit and you have given him dominion over your life, you can be confident in knowing that he has filled you according to his promise.

5. Be Faithful in Your Prayer Life

Let us then approach the throne of grace with confidence,
so that we may receive mercy and find grace to help us in our time of need.

Hebrews 4:16 NIV

What a privilege and a blessing to be given permission by God to approach his throne of grace, but what a shame that we often take this awesome opportunity for granted. God created us with an innate desire to be connected to him. When we fail to do so, an emptiness forms in our hearts, and our enemy is more than glad to fill it with things other than God.

God answers prayers, in his ways and in his timing. But, if we fail to pray, he has nothing to act upon.

Philippians 4:6–7 reads, "Don't worry about anything; instead, pray about everything. Tell God what you need, and thank him for all he has done. Then you will experience God's peace, which exceeds anything we can understand. His peace will guard your hearts and minds as you live in Christ Jesus."

6. Believe God Is Who He Says

When Jesus came to the region of Caesarea Philippi, he asked his disciples,
"Who do people say that the Son of Man is?"

"Well," they replied, "some say John the Baptist, some say Elijah, and others
say Jeremiah or one of the other prophets."

Then he asked them, "But who do you say I am?"

Simon Peter answered, "You are the Messiah, the Son of the living God."

Matthew 16:13–16

When life gets hard we tend to start doubting that God is God. We dabble with the lie that, just maybe, he isn't really in control. We wonder whether he is big enough to fix our problems. Or, at a minimum, we wonder whether he is taking time to see our problems at all. But God is who he says he is, all the time. In Revelation 1:8, God reminds us of who he is: "'I am the Alpha and the Omega—the beginning and the end,' says the Lord God. 'I am the one who is, who always was, and who is still to come—the Almighty One.'" God is always God, despite our circumstances.

What we view as God's absence or lack of quickness to change our circumstances or fix our problems is really God waiting for the proper time to act on our behalf, while simultaneously waiting for us to acknowledge our need for rescue.

Second Peter 3:9 says, "The Lord isn't really being slow about his promise, as some people think. No, he is being patient for your sake. He does not want anyone to be destroyed, but wants everyone to repent." If he "fixed" our problems overnight, would our love, dependency, and gratefulness for him really grow? We have to choose believe that God is God before he can act as God over our life.

Unbelief puts our circumstances between us and God; faith puts God between us and our circumstances. If you are serious about "resetting" your life, then let God be God in your life.

Reflection Questions

1. What steps can you take to realign your life to the Word of God? In what ways might you be out of step with his teachings and instructions?

2. What is your greatest need right now, either physically or emotionally? Do you trust that God can meet that need? Write a brief prayer confessing your dependency on God and committing to trust his ways and his timing.

3. In your desperation to manage your life and handle stress the best way you know how, have you become too self-sufficient? Do you need to surrender your life and your issues to God, giving him an opportunity to work in your life? Write down your thoughts here.

4. Have you really been filled with the Spirit, or have you just been playing a religious game of rituals and going through the motions?

5. If you have still not accepted Jesus Christ into your heart as your personal Savior, will you pause and do that right now? He has been waiting for you to discover that he is the answer you have been so desperately seeking. Your stress, anxiety, chaos, and busyness are merely symptoms of the absence of his hand in your life. He is standing with open arms, waiting to welcome you into his Kingdom. If your heart has been moved and you feel a desire and a need to truly invite Jesus into your life, will you say the prayer below? There is no right or wrong way to pray this prayer of salvation and commitment to Jesus. View this prayer as an opportunity to admit your need for God and invite him into your life without worrying over eloquent words or church sounding statements. Jesus is not concerned with how we talk to him or invite him in—just that we do.

Heavenly Father, have mercy on me, a sinner. I believe that you are the one true God. I believe the Holy Bible is infallible and that every word is true. I believe that Jesus Christ is the Son of the living God and that he died on the cross so that I may have forgiveness for my sins and eternal life in heaven. I know that without you in my heart, Lord, my life is meaningless and without purpose.

I believe in my heart that Jesus was raised from the dead and sits at your right hand. Please forgive me for every sin I have ever committed in thought or deed. Please come into my heart as my personal Lord and Savior today. I need you to be my Father, and I want you to be my best friend, fostering an intimate relationship with me.

I give you my life and ask you to take full control from this moment on. I am excited about the new life I will have in you. I pray all this in the name of Jesus Christ. Amen.

If you said this prayer today, welcome to the family of God. You have experienced a breakthrough, and your brokenness has made you whole.

(If you would like support and encouragement in your new relationship with Christ, please visit Proverbs 31 Ministries, at http://www.proverbs31.org/doyouknowJesus/doYouKnowJesus.php.)

Stress Busting Scriptures

For God so loved the world that he gave his one and only Son,
that whoever believes in him shall not perish but have eternal life.

John 3:16 NIV

Jesus answered, "I am the way and the truth and the life.
No one comes to the Father except through me."

John 14:6 NIV

For I will pour out water to quench your thirst
and to irrigate your parched fields.
And I will pour out my Spirit on your descendants,
and my blessing on your children.

Isaiah 44:3

Jesus replied, "I am the bread of life. Whoever comes to me will never be
hungry again. Whoever believes in me will never be thirsty."

John 6:35

And the Holy Spirit helps us in our weakness.
For example, we don't know what God wants us to pray for. But the Holy
Spirit prays for us with groanings that cannot be expressed in words.

Romans 8:26

Enjoying Your Stressed-Less Life

Let's pretend for a moment that my name is Martha and that I have a very large group of people coming over to my house for a dinner party, including a very special guest. I will make no plans for several days before the guests are supposed to arrive because I know my house will need a serious floor to roof cleaning—I'm going to be busy.

Tubs and toilets have rings around them that must be scrubbed and bleached. Carpets need to be vacuumed. But before any of this can be done, my children have a lot of work to do cleaning their rooms (so that the carpet actually becomes visible again) and picking up their myriad personal items that have been carelessly strewn about the house.

All the hardwood floors need a good hands-and-knees spot cleaning in preparation for the mopping and waxing that needs to take place. I decided long ago that my house is the dust magnet of the universe, so a lot of dusting will most certainly need to be done.

The window blinds have not been washed in so long that they are starting to look cream instead of white, and the stairs will need a good sweeping. I recently noticed that, when the sun shines in, it illuminates the fingerprints on the windows, so each of the windows needs to be cleaned.

The kids have dripped drinks and other liquid items down the kitchen cabinets, so all the cabinets will need to be wiped down, and a good coat of wood polish would even make them shine again.

The oven needs to be cleaned, since last week's lasagna drippings nearly caused a house fire. I noticed a few Christmas tree needles were still behind the couch, therefore, all the furniture will need to be moved so I can clean behind and under everything.

I definitely need to make sure that all the dirty clothes are washed and put away so that my laundry room will look as if I never use it (instead of its normal appearance implying that our family of five actually lives in it). Since the curtains in the house have not been washed in ten years, I probably should take them all down and wash and iron them.

The front porch needs to be swept. And the garage, too. But first I'll need to organize all the beach chairs, power tools, basketballs, bicycles, and muddy shoes that make the garage their home, just in case any of my guests want to enter my house through the garage door. If the weather is nice, my guests might want to venture outside for some fresh air, so I'd better sweep the deck, too. Oh yeah, and wipe down all of the deck furniture and then wash all the chair cushions.

Now for the exterior. I recently noticed that a few of our house shingles were loose, so I'll need to nag my husband to death and make his life miserable until he repairs them. I need to order ten bales of pine straw for the front lawn and get them laid out. I'm sure that new pansies around the mailbox would make a great impression when people approach the house, so I'll need to purchase and plant those and pull out all the weeds that have grown up over the winter (hopefully avoiding getting eaten by the fire ants that have overtaken the mailbox flower bed). The driveway could use a good pressure wash. Oh, and I need to make a mental note to call the boy who cuts the lawn.

After spending hours doing Internet searching, I will hopefully find several delectable gourmet recipes that I would probably never make for my own family. I'll type up my list and head to the grocery store. I'll need to add new kitchen towels to that list, since all the ones I have look as if they have spent some time in a blender. Then, when I get home, I will devote at least three hours to preparing appetizers and making sure they are strategically organized into glorious edible designs on the wedding china that has never been used. Then I will tackle the feat of cooking the main entrees.

On the day of the dinner party, I will surely be exhausted, to say the least. My family will be avoiding me by now for fear that I might ask them to do some form of house cleaning. And they will be terrified that they might accidentally spill their milk on my shiny, freshly waxed floors because that could cause a mommy meltdown.

When my guests finally arrive, including my very special guest, I will be thrilled! However, I will probably be too tired to get up and meet them at the door. I am sure they will marvel at how clean my house is and how wonderful my food looks and shower me with compliments and appreciation. And, if anyone who lives in my humble abode tries to sit around lazily and not help out while our guests are here, they better be ready for a tongue-lashing.

Then, after all that, hopefully I will still have enough energy left to sit with Jesus, my special guest. I'd love to talk quietly with him and soak in his peace and wisdom. But I imagine by that time I'll just be way too tired. Plus, I feel pretty confident I might already know the things he is going to talk about. I'm sure my body will feel like collapsing into a pile of mush from the overwhelming stress that I put myself through. But at least my day will have been productive with all my busyness, and the important thing is that everyone will be aware of how hard I worked. I will be the shining star at my own party. But maybe I'll have time for Jesus when the party is over. Or maybe the next day . . . or the next.

I can only imagine that the Martha we read about in the Bible, a friend of Jesus, may have felt this same way when Jesus and his seventy-two friends came to her house for a dinner party. Her chore list would certainly sound different than mine, considering that she lived in biblical times, but the overwhelming obsessive desire to make sure that everything was perfect was surely the same.

Instead of waxing the hard woods, she may have had to sweep all the dirt floors. And, instead of cleaning the blinds, she may have had to hand wash the burlap cloths hanging over the window openings. But, despite which chores she was focused on, it is obvious that she was focused on the chores, and possibly being fueled by an addiction to adrenaline, rather than quietly preparing to spend time with Jesus upon his arrival. Unfortunately, even after he arrived and she was in his presence, Martha still could not refrain from being busy and stressed.

We shouldn't be too hard on poor Martha and can't really blame her for feeling that way. After all, I feel sure that she wanted her house to be clean and her food to be delicious, just as I would. I have worn myself plum frazzled before when preparing for a party at my house. So, in the same way, she probably just wanted her guests to be pleased and her hard work to be noticed, just as I would. She wanted her busyness to be a sign of her dedication and her success to symbolize her importance, just as I would.

She wanted people to think she had the perfect home, the perfect family, and the perfect life. She wanted people to know how she had stressed over her preparations, so that they would appreciate her even more. She wanted to feel important. She wanted to know that she was doing a good thing—but what she didn't realize was that she was choosing the wrong "good thing." Jesus was the good thing. But she was too busy.

We live in a world where being an adrenaline junkie is considered a positive character trait. A world where we are expected to be all things to all people, juggling careers and families and daily pressure and crises, while keeping stress and anxiety at bay and maintaining the façade that we have it all together.

We are expected to push through our problems, pull ourselves up by our bootstraps, mask our emotions, and keep on trucking. We have been trained to believe we must keep going, and going, and going, like the Energizer bunny, without ever taking time to slow down, acknowledge our own needs, or worry about our stress level or our health.

Productivity becomes the indicator of our worth, and accomplishments drive our sense of purpose. We get trapped in the mindset of thinking that anxiety and depression are to be expected and accepted. And as a result of the demanding 24/7 culture we live in, we have come to believe that we have no choice but to succumb to a life of chaos—even if it means living a life void of any peace or joy.

We have been brainwashed by the world that stress is normal and that we are to live in that normal, whether we like or not. Worst of all, we convince ourselves that nothing can be done, but, in all honestly, nothing could be farther from the truth.

According to the words of Jesus, a stressed-out life is not at all the way we are called to live. In fact, it is exactly the opposite. Jesus calls us to choose something better.

The Choice Is Yours

Mary and Martha were sisters, and Lazarus was their brother. They all lived together in the town of Bethany, just a few miles outside of Jerusalem. The three of them were close friends of Jesus, which is why he chose to stay at their home the week before his crucifixion. According to the book of Luke, Martha was the head of this household, and she was the first one to welcome Jesus into her home. Mary was probably the younger sister, and, just like in every family since the beginning of time, sibling rivalry obviously existed.

Let's take a look at this story in Luke 10:38–42:

> As Jesus and his disciples were on their way, he came to a village where a woman named Martha opened her home to him. She had a sister called Mary, who sat at the Lord's feet listening to what he said. But Martha was distracted by all the preparations that had to be made. She came to him and asked, "Lord, don't you care that my sister has left me to do the work by myself? Tell her to help me!"
>
> "Martha, Martha," the Lord answered, "you are worried and upset about many things, but only one thing is needed. Mary

has chosen what is better, and it will not be taken away from her." (NIV)

Although Scripture doesn't say specifically, it is entirely possible (as is the case with most sisters) that Martha felt as if her little sister Mary had always been lazy, never helping around the house as much as she should, which resulted in her lack of patience at Mary's obvious negligence to help. Or perhaps Martha had already asked Mary several times to help her in the kitchen that day before she demanded that Jesus make Mary help.

This certainly happens in my house! It is a daily occurrence for my children to come to me and demand that I tell their sibling to do something. I often hear demands like, "Mom, tell her to take off my new shirt!" "Mom, tell him to give me my iPod back!" "Mom, tell her to come back and help me load the dishwasher!" "Mom, tell him to quit making obnoxious noises!"

So, in consideration of the fact that Jesus was the most respected guest in the house that day, Martha chose him as the one who would have the authority to force her sister to help her. I find it bewildering that she did not *ask* if Jesus would mind telling Mary to help, but instead she *demanded* that he tell her to help. Oh, have mercy, what was Martha thinking?! Did she not realize whom she was talking to?

Had her pride over her accomplishments poisoned her thoughts, causing her to think she was more important than others? Had her frustration and resentment caused her to forget that Jesus stood for peace and love, not tension and demands? Had her habit of busyness caused her to believe that being busy was better than taking time to talk with Jesus? Had the many distractions of her life clouded her mind, making her lose sight of the fact Jesus was the Son of God, not merely a houseguest? Had her perspective on what was most important in life been skewed because of the pressure she was under? Had Martha become so stressed that she had forgotten the importance of relaxing and enjoying life, trusting that Jesus had everything under control? Of course, we have no way of knowing what was really in Martha's heart or mind, but her actions seem to imply that the answer to each of these questions might be a resounding yes.

On the other hand, Mary did have the right perspective. She was apparently a woman who allowed her heart to guide her actions. In this story in Luke, we see her sitting at the feet of Jesus, even though chaos and busyness were swarming all around her. Later, in John 12:3, we see her anointing the feet of Jesus with expensive perfume, wiping it with her hair. Mary wanted to learn from Jesus, depend on Jesus, and sit in his presence, saturating her heart with the peace she knew Jesus offered, even if other people didn't "get it."

Martha, on the other hand, had become so involved in her stress, her duties, and her own agenda that she didn't have time to learn from, depend on, or sit with Jesus. As a result, Martha experienced stress instead of peace, because she was "worried and upset about many things."

The story about Martha and Mary ends after Jesus tells Martha that she is wrong and Mary is right. We are given no indication of whether the response from Jesus had a lasting impact on Martha's spirit. However, we can make sure that it has a lasting impact on us.

If you started out reading this book "worried and upset about many things," I pray that your heart has been changed to be more like Mary's and less like Martha's. I pray that you now have a heart that recognizes that Jesus is the answer to peace and serenity in a world characterized by chaos and stress.

Friends, my fervent prayer is that God has spoken loudly to your spirit and that, through the pages of this journey we have taken together, you have been transformed and peace has taken up residence in your heart.

I trust that God has moved in your life in ways that only he could do. And I hope that you have come to recognize the importance of turning your stress over to him. If you have come to a place where you can acknowledge God for who he really is, then you are in a position to consciously choose the "good thing" that is better than everything else, which can never be taken away.

Yet, despite how strong we may feel right now in our faith or how passionate we are about pursuing less stressed lives, the fact remains that life will continue on as normal. We have to acknowledge that with each passing day stumbling blocks will, without a doubt, roll into our paths. Difficult circumstances will threaten our peace, stressful situations may fly in like a swarm of angry bees, and existing and new problems may cause our faith to be stretched.

In our human frailty, it will be all too easy to default back into a habit of responding and reacting out of the flesh, allowing our emotions to cloud our thoughts, letting our stress become the stronghold over our lives rather than resting at the feet of Jesus in the midst of it all, as Mary did.

Although our peace can never be taken from us, we can relinquish it inadvertently when life gets difficult, circumstances seem hopeless, or the rush of adrenaline threatens to poison our hearts again. Let us take comfort in remembering that the Lord's mercies are renewed every day and that each new wave of peace is only a prayer away.

Lamentations 3:22–24: "The faithful love of the LORD never ends! His mercies never cease. Great is his faithfulness; his mercies begin afresh each morning. I say to myself, 'The LORD is my inheritance; therefore, I will hope in him!'"

Keeping in Step

Keeping our hearts in step with Jesus is the number one key to the stressed-less life. We cannot do this thing called life on our own, and he never intended for us to in the first place.

If we long to have a feeling of peace in our hearts, even when our earthly lives are far from peaceful, we must never forget to make Jesus the most important part of each day. He doesn't expect us to stay in perfect step with him, because that is obviously not possible in our sinful nature. But he calls us to do our best to mirror his footsteps and walk in his ways. He does not expect us to walk without stumbling, but he does want us to always look to him for help when we fall. In Ephesians 4:2–3 God offers a few tips for keeping our lives in step: "Be completely humble and gentle;

be patient, bearing with one another in love. Make every effort to keep the unity of the Spirit through the bond of peace" (NIV). And in Galatians 5:22–23, we see a few more ways to walk in his steps: "But the Holy Spirit produces this kind of fruit in our lives: love, joy, peace, patience, kindness, goodness, faithfulness, gentleness, and self-control. There is no law against these things!"

These verses portray the inner fruits that we need to harvest in our hearts if we desire for our outward actions to keep in step with what is important to Jesus. If our goal is to never return to a stressed, chaotic life void of joy and peace, then it's a good idea to pay close attention to God's suggestions. These fruits are the foundations for living the stressed-less life, and, once our hearts are in step with Jesus, the real journey to peace can begin.

Even though it may seem impossible to imagine, it is possible to trade in your stress for God's perfect peace. It may not happen overnight, but it will happen because, although your circumstances may be the same, your heart will not be.

Just like anything worth having, an intimate relationship with our Holy Savior takes devotion and dedication. A life that is less stressed takes a daily commitment of tapping into the spiritual strength of God so we can get through life without allowing it to get to us. If we are hungry for the peace that only God can provide, we must commit to doing whatever it takes to truly get to know the Prince of Peace.

As we focus on growing our relationship with him, we can still enjoy the positive stress-relief tactics that the world has to offer. Personally, I love a good massage, a relaxing pedicure, and a nap on the beach as the sounds of the surf soothe my soul. I love to romp in the spring grass with my children, exercise daily, take time to read a good novel, or listen to soft music. There is absolutely nothing wrong with enjoying things that make us feel rejuvenated and re-energized, and there is no need to feel guilty for enjoying life's simple pleasures. We just need to bear in mind that, no matter how good those things feel in the moment, they will always bring temporary peace, while real peace, the serenity that changes the course of our lives, will come from Jesus alone.

Isaiah 26:3 says "You will keep in perfect peace all who trust in you, all whose thoughts are fixed on you!" This verse sums up the entire message of this book in one sentence, because, when our minds are focused and fixed on Jesus and our lives are centered around trusting him every day in every circumstance, we will have a level of tranquility in our hearts and our minds that we never thought possible.

Friends, your life is not going to change because you read a book about stress. Your life is going to change when you realize that the absence of God in your life is intensifying the presence of stress in your heart.

Stress is an outward indication of an inner situation—a situation of a heart that needs Jesus. Only when we realize our need for him will we discover true peace in this less than peaceful world.

Life is complicated, but faith is not; and, upon embracing for yourself that Jesus is the only real solution for peace, you will be on the cusp of embarking upon your stressed-less life.

✒ Reflection Questions

1. What "chores" might be keeping you too busy for Jesus?

2. Have you ever felt too exhausted to spend time talking with Jesus? Explain a time where this happened, or admit if that describes your life right now.

3. Have you pushed Jesus to the back burner because daily responsibilities or stressors consumed all of your time? What changes can you make to ensure that Jesus is put at the top of your daily to-do list?

4. Consider the steps mentioned regarding staying in step with Jesus: humility, gentleness, patience, love, unity with God, joy, kindness, goodness, faithfulness, self-control. In what ways might you be "out of step" with Jesus? List them here.

5. Of the steps you listed above, which ones should you make a priority in your life right now? How would focusing on improving in these areas help you achieve peace?

6. If you were to insert your name into the questions pondered about Martha earlier in this chapter, what would your answers be? Jot your honest answers down after each question, and ask God to help you overcome any heart issues that might be preventing you from resting at his feet.

- Has pride over your accomplishments poisoned your thoughts, causing you to think you are more important than others?

- Has frustration and resentment caused you to forget that Jesus stands for peace and love, not tension and demands?

- Has your habit of busyness caused you to believe that being busy is better than spending downtime with Jesus and the people you love?

- Have the many distractions of your life clouded your mind, making you lose sight of the fact that Jesus is the Son of God? Are you taking him for granted?

- Has your perspective on what is most important in life been skewed because of the pressures you are under?

- Have you become so stressed because of your circumstances and overwhelming emotions that you have forgotten the importance of relaxing and enjoying life, trusting that Jesus has everything under control?

If your answer is "yes" to any or all of these questions, then know you need to make a commitment to set aside some quiet time in the next twenty-four hours for praying to God, seeking his face, asking for his guidance and perspective on the situations in your life, and searching for wisdom and clarity about the changes that you might need to make within yourself. Consider planning a miniretreat where you and God are the only attendees.

7. Do you now believe with your whole heart that Jesus is the only true solution for stress? Write a prayer of praise and thankfulness for the peace that Jesus offers, including your promise to always seek his face and keep your thoughts fixed on him, so that, when stress rises in your life, your peace will rise higher.

Stress Busting Scriptures

I wait quietly before God,
for my victory comes from him.
He alone is my rock and my salvation,
my fortress where I will never be shaken.

Psalm 62:1–2

The LORD says, "I will rescue those who love me.
I will protect those who trust in my name.
When they call on me, I will answer;
I will be with them in trouble.
I will rescue and honor them.
I will reward them with a long life
and give them my salvation."

Psalm 91:14–16

"But for you who fear my name,
the Sun of Righteousness will rise with healing in his wings.
And you will go free, leaping with joy like calves let out to pasture."

Malachi 4:2

The name of the LORD is a strong fortress;
the godly run to him and are safe.

Proverbs 18:10

"You are worried and upset about many things but,
only one thing is needed."

Luke 10:41b–42a NIV

Endnotes

1. "A Discussion of Stress: The Stress Epidemic," The StressFree Network, accessed October 21, 2011, http://www.stressfree.com/stress.html.

2. "APA Stress Survey: Deepening Concerns about Connection between Disease and Stress," *APA Practice Central,* January 26, 2012, http://www.apapracticecentral.org/update/2012/01-26/stress-survey. aspx?__utma=12968039.2050687443.1342280526.1342280526.134228 0526.1&__utmb=12968039.1.10.1342280526&__utmc=12968039&__ utmx=-&__utmz=12968039.1342280526.1.1.utmcsr=apapracticecentral. org|utmccn=(referral)|utmcmd=referral|utmcct=/&__utmv=-&__utmk=228529949.

3. R. A. Clay, "Stressed in America," *American Psychological Association,* January 2011, http://www.apa.org/monitor/2011/01/stressed-america.aspx.

4. "Employees Enter Holiday Season Stressed, Worried about Job Security," ComPsych Corporation, November 22, 2010, http://www.compsych.com/ press-room/press-releases-2010/353-nov-22-2010.

5. Clay, "Stressed in America."

6. "Stress in America," American Psychological Association, October 7, 2008, www.apa.org/news/press/releases/2008/10/stress-in-america.pdf.

7. Clay, "Stressed in America."

8. Sharon Jayson, "Americans are Stressed, but We're Getting Used to It" *USA Today,* January 11, 2012, http://yourlife. usatoday.com/health/medical/mentalhealth/story/2012-01-11/ Americans-are-stressed-but-were-getting-used-to-it/52485486/1.

9. Jayson, "Americans are Stressed."

10. Pam Belluck, "Obesity Rates Hit Plateau in U.S., Data Suggests," *New York Times,* January 13, 2010, http://www.nytimes.com/2010/01/14/health/14obese. html.

11. "Latest APA Survey Reveals Deepening Concerns About Connection Between Chronic Disease and Stress," American Psychological Association (Jan. 11, 2012), http://www.apa.org/news/press/releases/2012/01/chronic-disease.aspx.

12. "APA Stress Survey: Deepening Concerns."

13. "Stress Facts." The Health Resource Network. http://www.stresscure.com/hrn/facts.html.

14. Daniel K. Hall-Flavin, MD, "Chronic Stress: Can It Cause Depression?" Mayo Clinic, last modified March 27, 2012, http://www.mayoclinic.com/health/stress/AN01286.

15. "Stress Symptoms: Effects on Your Body, Feelings and Behavior," Mayo Clinic, last modified February 19, 2011, http://www.mayoclinic.com/health/stress-symptoms/SR00008_D.

16. "Stress a Major Health Problem in the U.S., Warns APA," American Psychological Association, October 24, 2007, http://www.apa.org/news/press/releases/2007/10/stress.aspx.

17. Denise Gellene, "Sleeping Pill Use Grows as Economy Keeps People Up at Night," *Los Angeles Times*, March 30, 2009, http://articles.latimes.com/2009/mar/30/health/he-sleep30.

18. Ron Ball, "Workplace Stress Sucks $300 Billion Annually from Corporate Profits," Technology Marketing Corporation, November 2004, http://www.tmcnet.com/call-center/1104/cccrm1.htm.

19. Beth Moore, *Mercy Triumphs* (Nashville, TN: Lifeway Church Resources, 2011), 78.

20. C. S. Lewis, *The Chronicles of Narnia: Prince Caspian* (New York: HarperTrophy, 1994), 141.

21. Max Lucado, *In The Eye Of The Storm* (Dallas, TX: Word, 1991), 54.

22. Elizabeth Scott, "The Definition of Epinephrine," About.com December 22, 2007, updated June 30, 2012, http://stress.about.com/od/stressmanagementglossary/g/Epinephrine.htm.

23. Krista Mahr, "How Stress Harms the Heart," *Time*, October 9, 2007, http://www.time.com/time/health/article/0,8599,1669766,00.html.

24. Joeann Fossland, "Are You Addicted To Adrenaline?" *RealtyTimes*, September 12, 2000, http://realtytimes.com/rtpages/20000912_adrenaline.htm.

25. Patrick Lencioni, "The Painful Reality of Adrenaline Addiction," *Leadership Review* 5 (2005): 3–6, http://www.leadershipreview.org/2005winter/LencioniArticle.pdf.

26. Logos Bible Software-*Holman Illustrated Bible Dictionary*, Holman Reference, p. 278.

27. John Launchbury, "Comment—God's Deeper Answer to Job—Part 1: The Beasts," *Tidings*, December 2004, http://www.tidings.org/studies/job200412.htm.

28. Glynnis Whitwer, "Who Do You Trust?" Proverbs 31 Ministries, August 2005, http://devotions.proverbs31.org.

Tracie Miles's passion is to help women live intentionally for Christ. In addition to being an author, Tracie is a national women's conference speaker and writer with Proverbs 31 Ministries. Through her genuine transparency, humor, and southern sincerity, Tracie speaks God's truths to empower and motivate women all over the country to depend on Christ in their everyday lives. She exhibits an enthusiastic desire to help women discover the fulfillment found in living a life focused on Christ so that they can find unshakable joy and peace.

Tracie lives with Michael, her husband of twenty-two years, and their three teenage children in Charlotte, North Carolina. In addition to being a Christian speaker and author, she is also a freelance corporate trainer for Fortune 500 companies, teaching stress management, leadership, and performance-improvement skills.

Invite Tracie to speak at your next women's event!

For more information, or to connect with Tracie,
visit her interactive website at:
www.traciewmiles.com

Proverbs 31 Ministries is an international ministry for women
that exists to bring peace, purpose, and perspective to today's
busy woman. It is like an online friend who will walk hand in
hand with you in your incredible adventure of faith.

To learn more about Proverbs 31 Ministries, visit our website at:
www.Proverbs31.org

Proverbs 31 Ministries
616-G Matthews-Mint Hill Road
Matthews, NC 28105

An Invitation From Tracie

If you were inspired by Stressed-less Living and would like to take your journey a step further, I want to invite you to visit my website to sign up for my free 10 Day Stress Detox to use as a devotional companion to the book.

I'd also love for you to take advantage of the free devotionals, stress management tips, and miscellaneous free resources to encourage you in keeping your stress at bay through Christ, and also for use in your small group or personal bible study.

www.traciewmiles.com

www.stressedlessliving.com